# THE EYE OF INTELLIGENCE

The author

# THE EYE OF
# INTELLIGENCE

URSULA POWYS-LYBBE

WILLIAM KIMBER · LONDON

First published in 1983 by
WILLIAM KIMBER & CO. LIMITED
Godolphin House, 22a Queen Anne's Gate,
London, SW1H 9AE

ISBN 0-7183-0468-3

Photoset in North Wales by
Derek Doyle & Associates, Mold, Clwyd
and printed in Great Britain by
Redwood Burn Limited,
Trowbridge, Wiltshire

# Contents

# List of Illustrations

*All photographs with the exception of the frontispiece and those on pages 37, 52 and 107 are Crown Copyright and appear by arrangement with the Public Record Office.*

# Foreword

by
Douglas N. Kendall
Wing Commander and Technical Control Officer
ACIU, RAF Medmenham

It is a great pleasure to be invited to write a brief forward to Ursula Powys-Lybbe's book on photographic intelligence.

Ursula was one of the photographic interpreters who joined the unit early in the war. She is writing, therefore, from personal knowledge. The unit, known initially as The Central Interpretation Unit and later as the Allied Central Interpretation Unit (ACIU for short) after the American organizations joined forces with it, consisted of 566 officers and 1186 other ranks. It included personnel from the British, American and Canadian forces of many types including the RAF, USAAF, British and Canadian armies, The Royal Navy, US Navy, US Marines, US Corps of Engineers and others.

The ACIU had a high priority in the recruitment of its staff. Experts were needed of many types. Typically, we were able to recruit the whole of the Archaeological Department from Cambridge on the theory that they were experienced in analysing data. It proved a happy choice.

Despite the many backgrounds of the interpreters and their affiliation with so many different military units, the ACIU operated very smoothly with complete integration of all personnel, irrespective of uniform or nationality. Sincere thanks are due to the whole staff for their efforts in making the system work.

It is not generally realized how big a volume of air photography was obtained. There were some 13 squadrons (5 RAF, 5 USAAF and 3 Canadian) whose sole function was to obtain air photography. In addition, every bomber, whether by night or day, carried a camera, as did the coastal patrol aircraft. All these photographs were sent to ACIU with minimum delay. The photographic coverage was so total and frequent that remarkably complete information could be deduced on many subjects.

Practically all British Intelligence sources collapsed in 1940 with the downfall of France. The UK was forced therefore to turn to air reconnaissance on an urgent and massive scale to replace the gap in information, this being the one source which the UK could control. Its contribution to operational intelligence was particularly important and no attack, whether a bombing raid, the landing of a few men on a beach or a massive landing of an army, was possible without the preparation of target information at ACIU. Also critical was the damage assessment following each bombing raid so that its effect could be analysed and the decision taken on whether to rebomb.

Air Photography is still of great importance today, and this is likely to continue for the foreseeable future.

D.N.K.

# Acknowledgements

Without the help and encouragement of my former colleagues it would have been impossible to complete this book which I regard not so much as mine, but as ours. During the three years of preparation, my recollections which had been notably absent, began to surge back as a result of my contacts with my friends, and even more so when, in an endeavour to soak up some atmosphere, I revisited Danesfield House, now magnificently restored to its former splendour by the new owners, Carnation Foods Company Ltd.

I am also greatly indebted to those on active service or recently retired from Her Majesty's armed forces who have given me so much friendly assistance. I wish I were able to include more names in the alphabetical list below, but space disallows it.

Constance Babington Smith, MBE (Babs); Bernard Babington Smith; Dr Winifred Bartindale; Lady (Charlotte) Bonham-Carter; David Brachi; R.H. Bulmer; Molly (Tommy) Chadsey; Professor Glyn Daniel; Geoffrey Deeley, MBE, FRBS; Professor Geoffrey Dimbleby; Professor George Dury; Captain Hamish Eaton, (Int. Corps); Norman Falcon, FRS; Gerry Feltham; John Garrett; Dr Ronald Gillanders; Eric Goodwin; John Holder; George Holleyman; Loyalty Howard; Douglas Kendal; André Kenny; Sir Peter Kent, D.Sc., FRS; Shirley (Eadon) Komrower; Paul Lamboit; Andrew Lyall; Squadron Leader Mike Mockford; Norman McCleod; Stella (Ogilvie) Palmer; Harold Pusey; Clive Rouse, MBE, FSA; Bill Seaby; George Schofield; Neil Simon; Ann Sentance Tapp; Peter (Waddy) Waddington; Captain Elie Weeks USAF (rtd); Bryan Westwood; Harry Williams; Anne Whiteman; Ted (Woody) Wood.

My thanks go also to: Mrs Eve Weston for permitting me to include an extract from the diary of Flt. Lt. Fane her late husband shot down during the war. Anthony Rota, the son of Bertram Rota for giving me access to his father's papers. Major W.W. Rostow for permitting me to include information from his EOU history; Charles Bardswell for his information regarding SOE and SIS landing and picking-up operations over enemy territory; Eric Goodwin for the loan of the Claude Wavell papers; M. le Vice-Admiral Herbout of the French Marine Nationale at Lorient for information regarding the port; Edward E. Thomas for his valued advice; members of the staff and personnel of the Ministry of Defence, the Public Records Office, JARIC (RAF Brampton), the RAF Museum, the Imperial War Museum, the Intelligence Corps Museum.

U.P.-L.

# Preface

For many years I had been thinking idly that it was perhaps time that one of our former photographic interpreters should produce a comprehensive history of the work undertaken at the Allied Central Interpretation Unit, RAF Medmenham in the Thames Valley, and that they should hurry up before those of us who remain became any older. I told myself that I was too involved with my own professional career to embark on such a project, and anyway I did not consider myself the most qualified person to do so. True, I had been one of the senior officers in the Women's Auxiliary Air Force engaged in the work, but I had been detached from the unit halfway through the war to join the planning staff in London of what was subsequently to be known as Operation Overlord or the Allied invasion of northern Europe. However, no such history appeared.

Then in 1978 two separate television channels transmitted similar programmes about the secret scientific war of World War Two, and I settled down to enjoy them as I suspected that Medmenham and perhaps some of my ex-colleagues would be included. I was disappointed, as the scientist taking the major role displayed, in my view, a marked lack of objectivity in his approach to the subject; moreover, in later published accounts, the competence of the interpretation officers is questioned. It was sufficient to galvanize me into action as I felt that the whole matter should be rectified and RAF Medmenham given its proper status as a branch of Military Intelligence.

My story is not a history of World War Two in general, but an account of a specialised branch of the armed services which has received comparatively little attention from writers. Important events that have been described in great detail elsewhere are not investigated in depth, as my endeavour is to bring into focus the viewpoint of the interpreters working as they did in conditions of great secrecy (even one from another) and, apart from a few senior officers at Medmenham, with little awareness of the wider spectrum of the war.

As I write, thirty-seven years have passed since the end of the war and inevitably research after such a period is not easy, as a large number of interpretation reports have been lost or are incomplete and many published accounts are at variance. Had it not been for the splendid support I have received from my friends, the former PI's,[1] who have trustingly loaned me accounts of their personal recollections and have suffered bombardments of my questions, I doubt whether I would have been able to complete the project.

The magicians at Bletchley Park, the headquarters of the Government Code and Cypher School, snatching intelligence out of the air as they decoded German cyphers encoded by means of their Enigma machine cypher, were in a much stronger position than we were vis-à-vis the authorities, as few would have the temerity to question the results of their secret methods. The basis for photographic intelligence, on the other hand, was the ordinary black and white photographic print familiar to the majority of people. It was therefore tempting for the recipients of Medmenham interpretation reports to borrow stereoscopic magnifiers and formulate their own opinions, sometimes overriding the findings of fully trained and experienced PI officers, particularly when the intelligence received was contrary to their expectations. In some cases our interpreters were 'invited' to rewrite their reports, an invitation which not unnaturally they refused.

The experiences of our German counterparts in this respect were inestimably worse. Their training, surprisingly, was much inferior to our own and they were not given officer rank, which meant that they held no authority, and if they made any errors, they might have found themselves in the equivalent of the 'glass-house' of the British army. According to prisoner-of-war interrogations, Top German Brass after receiving an interpretation report would stare at the accompanying aerial photographs through antiquated magnifying glasses and pass judgement, thereby foolishly throwing away one of the most important weapons essential in winning wars.

Owing to lack of space, I have had to confine the geographical area covered in the book to the Northern European Theatre of Operations, excluding those areas to which trained PI officers were

[1] The abbreviation PI indicates Photographic Interpreter or Photographic Interpretation.

posted such as the Middle East, India, and the Far East. Nor have I been able to include the work of the PI officers in the field attached to the Tactical Air Forces after the Allied troops had landed in France. For the same reason I could not record the exploits of the reconnaissance pilots whose skill and daring contributed the sensational photographs essential to our work. Regrettably also it has only been possible to include comparatively few names out of all those PI officers of whatever nationality who together combined to form the core of ACIU.

# CHAPTER ONE

# Pre-Medmenham Days

I spent the eight years before the war working hard as a professional photographer, first running a studio in Cairo and subsequently establishing a business in London known as the Touring Camera. The two projects fortunately were successful. About July 1939, becoming alarmed about the prospect of a future war, I decided to jettison the photography, and joined up in the Auxiliary Fire Service based at Chelsea. I then wangled a transfer to the Rosebery Avenue/Faringdon Road Fire Station to be nearer to friends in Fleet Street. My job as a driver was to ferry officials either of the London Fire Brigade or the AFS around London and the only time I ever smelt smoke was in answer to a call from a basement in South Kensington. This was during the winter of the 'phoney war', and it was not surprising that being nearly dead from boredom I chose to resign in the spring of 1940 and stay with friends who owned a charming sixteenth-century cottage in a little village in the Thames Valley. My idea was to do something useful to support the war effort (like raising chickens) and on no account ever to be seen in uniform again.

The little village, called Medmenham, was tucked into the foot of the Chilterns just where the land begins to slope away towards the river only a short distance down Ferry Lane. The church, Dog and Badger pub and the village shop were clustered round the crossroads on the main Henley to Marlow road, and they narrowly missed destruction from a stick of bombs dropped at random by the Luftwaffe during the summer of 1940. This was the first time I was to dive for shelter under a table.

One day, by an extraordinary coincidence considering what was to happen to me later, I happened to read a feature in a national newspaper about something called photographic interpretation. It described how marks on the ground when seen on aerial photographs might indicate enemy activity of vital importance to British Intelligence. When I had finished reading the article I knew without any doubt that PI was to be my future occupation. I cut out the article and filed it away.

A few days after I had put away my newspaper cutting, one of my friends informed us that a previous beau had just telephoned to say that he was in the district, and could he come to lunch? When he arrived, he was in the uniform of a wing commander and was wearing a black patch over one eye which he had lost as the result of a flying accident.

After making some joke about the eighteenth-century ruin at the end of Ferry Lane known as Medmenham Abbey, which had been created by Sir Francis Dashwood of West Wycombe for the irreligious junketings of his Hell-Fire Club, the Wing Commander told us that he had been searching for a house for the RAF, and had decided that the most suitable was Danesfield House, the vast white building overlooking miles of the River Thames from the top of the nearby hill. It had been built at the beginning of the century, mostly from local chalk, and the locals, considering it rather vulgar with its bogus Elizabethan chimneys and gothic ornamentation, christened it The Wedding Cake. The entrance to the drive was on the main road facing beautiful beech woods, later to afford concealment for RAF huts.

I produced my cutting, not realising that I was speaking to Wing Commander Hemming, Officer Commanding PDUI Photographic Development Unit Intelligence) based at Wembley, and asked if he could help me. He must have felt very surprised as he had made no mention of being connected in any way with the subject, and he informed me firmly that he could do nothing for me unless I enlisted in the Women's Auxiliary Air Force to serve my time in the ranks before going up for a course of photographic interpretation.

I would like to make the point here that photography as a profession had nothing whatsoever to do with photographic intelligence, and it was just a coincidence that I showed an aptitude for the work despite little or no mathematical ability.

My time in the ranks as a clerk in RAF Records at Ruislip from the beginning of January 1941 was endured by the thought of Wing Commander Hemming and his promise to help, but by the end of two months I began to have doubts. The only excitement that my fellow workers and myself experienced was the moment when a cheeky German fighter pilot raked our huts with machine gun fire, and I found myself sheltering under a table for the second time. Then came the blessed relief of being summoned to Wembley for my PI course which I managed to pass. The job automatically held an officer's commission, so after a short spell of leave during which I got myself kitted out in WAAF officer's uniform with the rank of Assistant Section Officer (the lowest possible) I joined the newly established Central Interpretation Unit at Medmenham on 1st April 1941.

The well-documented early history of aerial photography takes us back to the time of that dedicated Frenchman and professional photographer Felix Tournachon (Nadar) who in 1845 photographed Paris from the skies, climbing into the basket of a balloon which acted as the first 'flying platform' for an aerial camera. As camera design improved so camera-carrying balloons were used more frequently particularly in times of war and later to be superseded by another type of flying platform – the aeroplane. Stereoscopic slides taken from ground level were employed for map making in quite early days.

During World War One, excellent quality prints were achieved and even the small scale did not preclude quite advanced interpretation. Military maps were brought up to date with the aid of photography, the network of enemy trenches could be traced, camouflage was detected, the position of gun batteries plotted, and even the generators of poison gas were identified. By 1917 interpreters were sufficiently experienced to be able to calculate the rise and fall of tides.

The name of Hugh Hamshaw-Thomas, known to everyone connected with PI in World War Two, comes into our story for the first time when as a young lieutenant in the Royal Field Artillery, he becomes a photographic officer with the Royal Flying Corps Wing attached to 5 Corps in 1917, and which was to operate in the Middle East. There he was responsible for the reproduction of maps drawn from aerial photographs of the Battle of Gaza to the scale of 1:40,000, and despite lack of specialised equipment, went on to map the whole of southern Palestine from photographs taken by No 67 (Australian) Squadron to the scale of 1:20,000.

By the end of the Great War the RFC was superseded by the Royal Air Force, and established as an independent Service producing, as one of their tasks, aerial photographs to be passed on to the Army PI's for interpretation reports or for map-making.

It would be logical to assume that this newest and successful branch of military intelligence would have been maintained at a reasonably high level during the years of peace, but this was not to be. Most of the skills and techniques were lost and had to be re-learned, and had it not been for a few enthusiasts giving lectures on the practical application of photographic interpretation to military and civilian enterprises it might well have died.

The RAF School of Photography at Farnborough continued to train photographic officers, and in 1925 it was decided to include some instruction on PI in the curriculum. An army officer was appointed to establish the course which was designed to teach the art to regimental and battalion officers. Ten years later, in 1935, Captain T.B.L. Churchill, the instructor, had to spend useful time salvaging stereoscopic equipment left over from World War One because the War Office, probably badgered by the Treasury, refused to supply new stereo magnifiers. It could be said that Captain Churchill was responsible for laying the foundation for the training required in the forthcoming war.

It was fortunate that the value of PI was realised in 1938 by those who correctly forecast that the time which would elapse before the outbreak of hostilities was becoming precariously shorter, and at last some action was taken. A special section was created in the Directorate of Intelligence known as AIl(h) to further PI operations, attendance at Farnborough was stepped up to include short courses for intelligence officers of the army and RAF, and an updated manual of instruction appeared. In the summer of 1938 that famous Australian pilot and entrepreneur Sidney Cotton was asked to act for British Intelligence. His brief was to fly clandestine sorties over Germany as international regulations precluded any over-flying reconnaissance. He concealed Leica cameras about his aeroplane and while acting the part of a rich businessman with interests in Germany, set about photographing German military installations and anything else useful to our cause. Without Cotton's tactics and without the help offered by a small civilian aerial survey company known as the Air Operating Company of Wembley, the years of war might well have been prolonged. As it was, British Intelligence was able to benefit from accurate information contributing to some extent to an assessment of the German war potential.

When war was declared in September 1939 and the strength of establishments could be assessed, the inadequate numbers of trained PI officers must have come as a great shock to the authorities. There was one RAF officer at Air Ministry AIl(h), six

RAF officers at Bomber Command under Flight Lieutenant Peter Riddell, one Army officer at the school at Farnborough and none in Naval Intelligence. Fortunately there were a number of IO's (Intelligence Officers) of both the Army and the RAF who had passed the short course and had been posted to RAF stations – they at least had basic knowledge.

On the reconnaissance side, six squadrons from No 2 Group Bomber Command, flying Blenheim aircraft in which cameras had been installed, possessed photographic staff for processing film and prints, and a few interpreters were included on the strength. The outlook was not good.

On the day war was declared, at 1200 hours Blenheim No 6215 of 139 Squadron based at RAF Wyton piloted by Flying Officer McPherson with a crew consisting of Commander Thompson RN (observer) and Corporal Arrowsmith, took off from Wyton on the first photographic mission of the war and was the first aircraft to cross enemy territory. Their brief was to photograph the German warships lying in the Schillig Roads off Wilhelmshaven, which had already been covered by one of Cotton's pilots the previous day. Approximately four hours later the aircraft returned with photographs of excellent quality and the location of the warships was again confirmed.

Subsequent sorties flown from Wyton were not so successful as no fewer than eight Blenheims of No 2 Group were shot down, and there were camera failures. Losses were even greater when, from October 1939 No 53 Squadron and later 70 Wing (No 18 and No 57 Squadrons) operated from France, and more than twenty were shot out of the sky in the first early months.

In desperation Air Ministry turned to Sidney Cotton who, from his previous experience with his clandestine missions, knew exactly what was required to save the situation. The result was the selection of the Spitfire cleaned up by Cotton for extra speed and ceiling, and range and he was authorised to form a unit within the RAF based at Heston airfield on 15th September 1939; the unit to be known as the 'Heston Special Flight'. He was given the rank of wing commander and a small number of RAF personnel were assigned to him as well as two Spitfires in exchange for 'cottonizing' Blenheims of Fighter Command. His own Lockheed and Beechcraft were also available for duty, and the Special Flight came under the auspices of the newly named Photographic Development Unit (PDU) at Heston.

At the beginning of November 1939 a detachment of the Special Flight moved to Seclin airfield near Lille and from there and other airfields a large area of Germany was photographed; Cologne, Düsseldorf, Kaiserslautern and Wiesbaden were some of the cities covered. The photographic sorties were an immediate success, but then came a hitch. Air Ministry AI1(h) found that they were unable to keep up with the requirements for PI and furthermore they found they had insurmountable problems obtaining detailed information from the very small scale photographs. Something had to be done and Wing Commander Cotton again came to the rescue.

Major Lemnos Hemming, managing director of the small air survey company called the Air Operating Company (AOC) of Wembley, had previously offered the company's premises, use of cameras and the expertise of his staff to the Admiralty, Air Ministry, the War Office and the Foreign Office in turn, only to be rejected. Major Hemming also happened to be a close friend of Sidney Cotton, who immediately approached him with Air Ministry's problem and was given the availability of all the assets declined by the Admiralty, Air Ministry, the War Office and the Foreign Office. A close liaison was formed between AOC and the Heston Special Flight, and the entire staff at Wembley was placed at Cotton's disposal without any official contract.

Here I must return briefly to the fortunes of the army interpreters who were already in France with the BEF. A new section, GSIa(v), was added to the intelligence branch of GHQ to deal with PI and was based at the village of Habacq, near Arras GHQ. A good working relationship was established with their opposite numbers at the French Deuxième Bureau at Meaux, and in November and December of 1939, Major Churchill (formerly at Farnborough) ran two courses of PI at Arras.

It was at this time that Douglas Kendall, who was to take such an important role in the history of PI, approached Major Hemming.

This young man, whose home was in Portugal because of his family's business concerns, became interested in air survey and was introduced to Major Hemming who then controlled the Air Operating Company of South Africa. Douglas took a course in surveying and elementary geodetics, he obtained a pilot's certificate at Hatfield and joined the company in South Africa before the war. There he learned the business thoroughly including darkroom work, mapping and photogrammetry, and when the company

First PR flight by Mark I Spitfire carrying two F24 5″ cameras in place of armament. Wing Commander Sidney Cotton O/C No 2 Camouflage Unit Heston and Flight Lieutenant M.V. Longbottom, the pilot. 20th November 1939.

The memorable sortie of 2nd March 1940 when almost the whole of the Ruhr Valley was photographed at a scale of 1:45,000 by a pilot of the Special Flight — the resulting mosaic was still being used in 1944 for standard briefing.

started to participate in air survey projects involving forestry, soil erosion and geology, Douglas returned to England for further courses in botany, foresty and road alignment: all these subjects preparing him for the special tasks of the future.

War was declared when he was spending a vacation in Portugal, so with great difficulty because of the paucity of transport, he reached England for the sole purpose of re-making the acquaintance of Lemnos Hemming. Inevitably he met Sidney Cotton who got him a commission in the Royal Air Force with the rank of pilot officer in the Heston Special Flight which in January 1940 was renamed the Photographic Development Unit (PDU).

Two weeks after he had joined, Wing Commander Cotton's newest pilot officer was posted to France to attend a course of PI at the Deuxième Bureau. Here he was taught the basic skills of the art and spent most of his time studying photographs of the Siegfried Line and identifying gun emplacements. After the course he joined 212 Squadron, then established with its photographic section at Tigeaux, close to Air Marshal Sir Arthur Barratt's HQ at Coulommiers, and to the Deuxième Bureau at Meaux; he was to stay at Meaux until the time came in May 1940 to get out fast before the advancing German army.

No 212 Squadron was formed under the auspices of PDU in January 1940 under the operational control of AOC-in-C of British Air Forces in France (BAFF) Air Marshal Sir Arthur Barratt, and the Squadron HQ staff included seven intelligence officers responsible for interpretation and plotting, a photographic officer and forty other ranks for processing and printing.

Photographic print libraries were being gradually built up at Heston, and AI1(h) was still struggling to interpret small scale prints, although the solution to that particular problem was held at the Air Operating Company in the shape of a mechanical stereoscopic plotter known as the 'Wild' machine (pronounced 'Vilt' being of Swiss origin). Briefly, the function of this machine was to make maps utilizing photographs, and it was now discovered that it was capable of obtaining the measurements of ships and to draw large scale plans of docks, for example. Small scale prints presented it with no problem.

In February 1940 an event of the very greatest importance occurred in the world of the interpreters which was to affect the whole future of the embryo PI branch of Intelligence. The Admiralty, having become more and more disenchanted with the visual reconnaissance provided by Coastal Command, desperately needed confirmation of reports that the battleship *Tirpitz* had left dry dock at Wilhelmshaven and was probably operational. So on 10th February 1940 a successful sortie was flown over the port, only to be rejected by AI1(h) as being of no intelligence value because of the smallness of scale. Thereupon Wing Commander Cotton took the photographs over to his friends at AOC Wembley to see what the Wild machine could do for him. Michael Spender, an experienced photogrammetrist, and Wild operator, experimented with the 1:80,000 scale prints, and in spite of considerable tilt caused at the actual moment of exposure, managed to interpret the prints and was able to report to the Admiralty that the *Tirpitz* was still safely in dry dock.

Two days later Michael produced beautifully accurate plans of the port including the shipping at a scale of 1:25,000. The First Sea Lord, Winston Churchill, saw and admired the plans and then discovered that the work had been undertaken unofficially. He wrote to Sir Kingsley Wood, Secretary of State for Air, to the effect that if Air Ministry did not wish to take over the stereoscopic arrangement possessed by Major Hemming's organisation, the Admiralty would do so. That was enough for Air Ministry who almost immediately began negotiations with the Air Operating Company. However it was not until May that an agreement was achieved, back-dated to 1st April 1940, and Major Lemnos Hemming was given the rank of wing commander in charge.

On the night of 19th/20th March 1940 the first bombing attack was made on German territory. Hornum seaplane base on the island of Sylt was the target for this particular mission which was mounted in retaliation for the German attack on Scapa Flow, and it was also known that mine-laying aircraft operated from the island.

Once the crews had returned safely, the Prime Minister, Neville Chamberlain, gave out the information in a speech in the House of Commons and banner headlines screamed the news of the total destruction of the seaplane base, at the same time contradicting German reports that the bombs had been dropped on Denmark – statements which, the British press claimed, were to give the impression that Bomber Command had failed in the mission.

There was general euphoria in all circles except at Bomber Command where personnel waited holding their breath for the results of the interpretation of the post-strike photographs hoping that devastating damage would be revealed. However, it was the duty of the unfortunate flight lieutenant in charge of the PI section at HQ Bomber Command, Peter Riddell (later to become a group captain) to have to report that there was no damage whatsoever to be seen and not even one bomb crater.

The resulting furore can be imagined. Here was some miserable flight lieutenant in charge of a section of near-idiots having the nerve to insist that not one aircraft out of forty had reached the target even though aircrew had all confirmed the success of the mission, and this bunch of cretins was responsible for the whole establishment from the Prime Minister down, ending up with egg on their faces.

It is a moot point whether it was the C-in-C, Air Chief Marshal Sir Edgar Ludlow-Hewitt or Group Captain Arthur Harris in command of No 5 Bomber Group who gave the order that Peter Riddell and his PI's were to be locked in their room until they found signs of damage. There is much variance in the story but there is no doubt that that part of it was true. Peter managed somehow to get the photographs to AI1(h) who confirmed his report, but Harris, still unbelieving, ordered a reconnaissance aircraft to fly over Sylt to obtain low-level obliques. The result was the same – not a sign of damage or bomb craters. It was established from later photographs that a Danish island had received the bomb loads.

This sad story again illustrates the extraordinary pressures that were applied to interpreters on occasions, and which needed very great firmness and self-reliance to withstand, and I have a particularly vivid account from Stella Palmer, one of the WAAF officers at Bomber Command:

> We were constantly being pressurized by the Station Commander to publish glowing reports of glorious successes. If the interpreters found no trace of damage or craters, they were accused of minimising the results and our unfortunate officer in charge received hell – no one believed in our reports, and our reputation was nil. The worst of it was, so often no damage existed, and bomber crews had to be told the truth. Can you imagine our feelings?
>
> To begin with, they hated taking night photographs as operating the cameras meant just one more headache during a period of great danger, and they always had the thought of carrying with them in the aircraft a large amount of flammable material in the form of film, which they would be unable to discharge in an emergency. The photographic flash was the responsibility of the bomb aimer, and the method of

launching the flash was primitive. They might have to consult out-dated maps of, for example, miles and miles of featureless Dutch polder-country made up of interminable canals, and trace their position by some group of willows, or a kink in a dyke, and desperately try to plot craters by the bomb flashes. Half the time they were lost, as navigational aids and bomb aiming devices were of the crudest. It was tragic when they managed to stagger back with dead or wounded only to be told that they had been nowhere near the target by what they considered to be a bunch of idiots. We longed to be able to see successful results and hear their relieved and excited remarks.

There were further examples of unsuccessful bombing with post-strike claims of accuracy, such as the attack on Mannheim in December 1940 by 102 bomber crews. Photographs revealed that although there had been considerable damage, a large number of bombs had not reached the target; and again on 24th December 1940, photographs showed that only a few bomb craters could be plotted within the target area, after the raid on the synthetic oil refinery at Gelsenkirchen, when about 1,000 bombs had been dropped. It was not a question of the craters being found just outside the target area, but at a very long distance away.

When the photographs had shown how little damage was achieved with so great an effort, Professor Lindemann, personal scientific adviser to the Prime Minister, Winston Churchill, approached him, with his fears as to the accuracy of the navigation; Professor Glyn Daniel, then an interpreter at CIU, recalls that he and Douglas Kendall were summoned to Professor Lindemann in order to brief him with an analysis of bombing operations in relation to navigational accuracy.

The information given to the Prime Minister activated an immediate reaction, and experimentation was undertaken with regard to radio aids to navigation, such as $H_2S$ and Oboe; and a device known as Gee which was in a very early stage of development. $H_2S$ was a method of navigation by the use of a radar screen inside the aircraft. As both Gee and Oboe were limited by the range of radio transmission, the idea was that the bomber should first navigate with the aid of Gee or other methods, and then, at about fifty miles from the target, the pilot was to switch on the $H_2S$ and drop the bombs through cloud or haze without any jamming or interference. As Winston Churchill remarked: 'Distance would not matter, as the aircraft would carry its radar eye with it, wherever it went, and the eye could see in the dark'. In those days, of course, the system of radar was not known as such until 1943 when the H$_2$S equipment was ready for action.

Another extremely important event had occurred on 7th April 1940, this time stressing the vital significance of comparative sorties when making an interpretation report. The Admiralty had for the first time requested Kiel to be photographed. The sortie was undertaken by an extra long-range Spitfire and the interpreters reported that a very large amount of shipping could be seen in or near the port, and that numbers and numbers of Ju52s transport aircraft had been parked on Holtenau airfield nearby. The explanation of all this activity was the preparation for the invasion of Denmark and Norway two days later, but as there were no previous sorties available for comparison, it was impossible to foretell this from the photographs. The authorities considered that the PIs had failed in not realising that there was a reason for the activity.

In mid-May after the outbreak of the blitzkrieg the Germans broke through into France at Sedan and it was left to Douglas Kendall at Meaux to interpret the photographs taken by 212 Squadron operating from the airfield near Tigeaux in the heart of the Brie country. Their French colleagues had all left, so after a few days, having received no orders to move, he joined up with the squadron to be nearer to the photographic unit in their mobile trailers.

Having commandeered a small château at Tigeaux, the two hundred personnel of the squadron stayed there right through May until the fall of Paris on 14th June 1940. Deeming it healthier to push south towards Poitiers and continuing to retreat westwards in the direction of La Rochelle, the party, consisting of two or three RAF officers (the numbers are not clear) with NCOs and the remainder other ranks, set off with sufficient vehicles to transport all personnel with the mobile trailers and all the equipment. They had two Spitfires and a Lockheed Hudson with them and every day they overloaded the Hudson so that the troops could be returned to England and Heston.

By 16th June 1940 their numbers had dwindled to twenty and they had managed to reach a small airfield at Fontenay-le-Comte inland from La Rochelle when they heard the news of the German rate of advance – an anxious moment as they realised that soon there must be nothing but enemy territory between them and the Channel coast, and if, as seemed likely, France capitulated they could not

Preparation for the invasion of Denmark and Norway. Shipping in Kiel Harbour and Ju52 transport aircraft on Holtenau airfield can be seen. Because of lack of earlier cover, PI's had no way of knowing that numbers were unusually large.

expect the Hudson to make any return journeys.

By a great stroke of luck they had picked up a battered and abandoned Fairey Battle with a big dent in one wing where it had hit a tree and they cleverly got it airborne again. Two de Havilland Tiger Moths were found and salvaged as well. About eight people were stuffed into the Fairey Battle lying all over each other in the bomb bay, and all arrived safely in England. The Tiger Moths were more of a problem as they did not have sufficient range for the journey home, but nothing daunted, a pilot was put in each and the front seats loaded with petrol cans. The idea was to fly to Brest Peninsula, land in a field, refuel and press on; this they did, both aircraft completing the flight successfully.

Sidney Cotton caught up with his dwindling squadron in the early hours of 17th June 1940, when he landed his aeroplane. He took off almost immediately, announcing he would fly to Bordeaux, and find a suitable aircraft to lift them out, and that he would be back by 11.00 hrs.

By four o'clock, Cotton still had not turned up, so the group decided that the only thing to be done was to put a match to all the vehicles (except four in which to reach the coast), and the mobile photographic trailers. It must have been a grim moment watching the bonfire of such valued possessions before they hurried away to La Rochelle in search of a sea passage.

With mixed feelings, they spotted Cotton's aircraft arriving at Fontenay-le-Comte, and the last car in the convoy, which included Douglas Kendall, turned back for the airfield while the others continued. When the wing commander came in to land with an aircraft full to overflowing with British civilians whom he had picked up, he informed Douglas that another aircraft was to land shortly, and fuel would have to be found for it. They all pointed to a column of oily black smoke which infuriated Cotton so much that he took off for England with all his passengers.

Douglas and his companions hung around until a troop carrier aircraft capable of lifting eight people duly landed, and they piled in hoping to reach Nantes with whatever was left in the tanks. Fortunately they made it, managing to scrounge enough petrol to take them to the Channel Islands, finally to land back at Heston the following day, 18th June 1940.

This adventure proved to be a disaster where Sidney Cotton's future service career was concerned as he had been ordered to evacuate his squadron some weeks previously. He thought he knew better, never believing for one moment that France would fall; instead all the equipment was lost and the members of 212 Squadron narrowly missed capture or being shot down. It was the last straw for Air Ministry who had already found Cotton's unorthodox and independent methods extremely trying, brilliant though they may have been. He was replaced later by Wing Commander Tuttle who became commanding officer at PDU Heston.

Because of the German advance, the army PIs of GSIa(v) in their village of Habacq near Arras also had to be evacuated in a great hurry and arrangements were made to remove precious photographic material to safety. They found themselves in as equally an unnerving position as their colleagues of the RAF. A Buick Century staff car was loaded with all the negatives held by the section, and Captain Yool with one RAF officer and an army corporal were entrusted with the valuable cargo. They reached Boulogne, and after roaming about the town came to the conclusion that their Intelligence branch would never again be established in France. They were successful in shipping the negatives across the Channel and later joined the evacuation from Dunkirk during 26th May to 4th June.

Major Venour and Captain Lacoste took charge of the section's store of maps and prints and also reached Boulogne only to find that the Germans were advancing so rapidly that it was considered wiser to push on to Wimereux. In the grounds of a civilian hospital they began the almost impossible task of burning thousands of maps and aerial photographs. It took considerable time as layer upon layer of carbon became fire resistant to the layer below.

Eventually they made their way to the north-east as they had heard that the BEF was withdrawing either to Ostend or Dunkirk and the enemy tanks were not far distant. Fortunately many of these had run out of ammunition, while others had to be abandoned because of the attentions of patriotic Frenchmen dropping sugar into the fuel tanks. Both PI officers reached home safely via Dunkirk.

In the meantime the former AOC aerial survey company at Wembley had been undergoing major changes in order to be able to deal with the mountains of work now required of them by Wing Commander Cotton's requests for interpretation. The subjects were becoming more specialised as photography improved and as the range of reconnaissance aircraft extended, and the knowledge of the interpreters broadened, AI1(h), the Air Ministry Intelligence Department dealing with PI, moved into the company's premises in April 1940 and the offices became known as PADUOC House (anagram of PDUAOC). AI1(h) was absorbed into the organisation when Wing Commander Cotton was placed in command.

The control of PDU was shuffled around from authority to authority from the time Air Ministry placed it under the Directorate of Intelligence on 21st May 1940 and under Coastal Command for administration. There was acrimony from Bomber Command who was desirous of obtaining partial control, but by July 1940 the organisation was fairly stable. PDU had been split into two, the reconnaissance side being known as Photographic Reconnaissance Unit (PRU) with Wing Commander Tuttle in command, and the interpretation side (PIU) under Squadron Leader (former Major) Hemming. Interpretation had been centralised, with the exception of HQ Bomber Command retaining its separate bomb damage assessment section. Both PRU and PIU were to remain under Coastal Command for administration.

PADUOC House was rapidly taking the shape of the Central Interpretation Unit of the future: the early establishment of PIU consisted of nineteen RAF officers, eighteen WAAF officers, sixty-nine RAF airmen and eight WAAF other ranks. Squadron Leader Peter Riddell had been posted to the unit from Bomber Command and was to create the successful 'phase' system of interpretation; while the specialised sections dealing with German airfields, navy and shipping, army subjects, radar, camouflage, began to be set up. The photogrammetrists with the Wild machine continued in their important role of offering support to the interpreters' reports. Nearly all the sections described later in this book had been created by January 1941. In August 1940 the first course of photographic interpretation took place at PIU.

The army interpreters, immediately after the fall of France, consisted of only four officers who faced the almost impossible task of dealing with all the requirements from the War Office and elsewhere. Their cries for help were finally answered in August 1940 when the C-in-C Home Forces announced rather stuffily that as RAF interpreters were not trained in army requirements, nor in the recognition of objects of military importance, the need for an adequately trained and skilled Army Interpretation Unit at

Invasion Barges. (Dotted lines indicate barge concentration in the ports of Calais, Dunkirk and Boulogne.) (*Top left*) Calais 3rd September 1940 — no barges. (*Top right*) Calais 17th September 1940 — 266 barges. (*Bottom left*) Dunkirk 17th September 1940 — 220 barges. (*Bottom right*) Boulogne 18th September 1940 — 230 barges.

Wembley had become apparent. So it was in September 1940 that the Army Photographic Interpretation Section (thenceforth known as APIS), with an establishment of one GS02, three GS03s and eighteen IOs, was formed under the control of GHQ Home Forces but within the framework of the RAF PIU. Curiously I have come across no record of naval interpretation officers at Wembley at that time, only mention of naval liaison officers.

The main tasks of PIU in 1940 were the constant surveillance of the German naval units, and when the threat of invasion became apparent, the identification of up to a thousand converted invasion barges for troop landings seen in the Channel ports or moving down the canals and along the coast. This meant the counting of barges and more barges every day, and it was this information that finally led to the warning on 6th September 1940 that the invasion of Britain was imminent (code-named Sea-Lion).

Airfields also were constantly watched to assess their development and the order of battle of the Luftwaffe, while the tasks of APIS were to identify and plot on their military maps all the coastal gun batteries and other military installations, and note the movement of the German troops. The radar section under Squadron Leader Claude Wavell showed great promise very early by being able to confirm from photographs that radar was being used by the enemy when the section identified a Knickebein Navigational Beam station, and noticed that the aerial array was actually rotating.

Since the days of tactical warfare before the fall of France, strategic planning had been in operation, with the result that more detailed information was required from the interpreters, which in its turn created the need for the specialised sections included in the PIU organization. Reconnaissance aircraft were being improved and developed both in design and performance so that the eyes of our Intelligence on their flying platforms were able to probe deeper and further into enemy territory, just as its ears became more and more attuned to the deciphering of the secret codes of the German Enigma machine cypher. Britain was isolated from conventional intelligence from Europe after Dunkirk but reports started to trickle through again as and when our agents became operational, and air crews of the Luftwaffe shot down over England contributed information.

The importance of all branches of intelligence becoming interdependent was vital, and this aspect of the war has often been overlooked in books dealing with the subject. Many have been written describing a single facet of it, such as Ultra and Enigma or the bravery of agents living and working within the occupied countries. Aerial photography and its subsequent interpretation was a source of intelligence second to none as it was factual; it was capable of recording an event, not only when it occurred but also the results, such as an attack by Bomber Command and the aftermath of bomb damage. It could supply fresh and accurate news of enemy strategic planning, whether of the army, air force or German navy, and it was welcomed as an equal partner with other branches. The basis of all intelligence is cross-checking and all three of the British armed services and the United States possessed intelligence departments where data was collected and re-issued.

By 1942 a system was established whereby the Special Intelligence Service (SIS) reports were distributed to the Central Interpretation Unit at Medmenham for cross-checking against photographic evidence. I can give a small example of this work when a rough sketch of a German operational airfield which had been smuggled into the country came into my own airfield section. Much of the sketch was inaccurate, probably because the agent had insufficient knowledge of the subject or was not able to approach close enough, or indeed it might have been of German origin. Conversely if the agent's reports were found to be accurate, the integrity of the source could be established.

There was a reciprocal flow of intelligence between Bletchley Park where the Enigma machine was decoded and Medmenham, each being able to contribute information to the other. This activity was unknown to the PIs, as it was only handled by Douglas Kendall. In some cases intelligence was withheld from the interpretation unit, on the grounds that it was dangerous to share certain information, thus depriving the interpreters of material vital for the success of their work.

CHAPTER TWO

# The Power House
# and how it worked

Both the PRU at Heston and PIU at Wembley suffered the attentions of the Luftwaffe during the raids of August and September 1940 and both establishments were severely damaged with the loss of three Spitfires and a Lockheed. One of my first impressions in PADUOC House was of a large number of buckets placed in strategic positions to catch rainwater from the leaking roof. Umbrellas were sometimes as essential to the interpreters in their work as were their stereos.

A new operational base for the aircraft was chosen at Benson near Oxford to be known as No 1 PRU, and it was then that Wing Commander Hemming was touring the Home Counties in search of his house for the RAF; obviously the interpreters could not be left on their own divorced from PRU and with their premises being demolished around their ears. As we have seen, Danesfield House at Medmenham became their new base and the centre of the whole reconnaissance and interpretation organisation. This had been given the title of the Central Interpretation Unit, (CIU) in January 1941 and, perhaps confusingly, became known as the Allied Central Interpretation Unit (ACIU) when the Americans officially became part of the unit in May 1944 even though PIs of the US army had been working in with APIS since January 1944.

As the structure of the organisation underwent a number of changes during the war, I think it would be more profitable to concentrate on the period of maximum output in 1944-1945 to give some idea of how ACIU was able to cope with the enormous work-load.

It can be seen from the chart on page 39 that there was a two-way flow of information to and from the unit; demand on the one hand from the 'customers', i.e. the Admiralty (fifteen departments), the War Office (thirteen), Air Ministry (thirty), the Ministry of Economic Warfare, Navy, Army and Air Force Commands, SHAEF, Overseas Commands and more. All interpretation reports on the other hand were supplied direct to the 'customers'. The various interpretation sections were fed from

Danesfield House. (*Taken by USAAF 325th Reconnaissance Wing.*)

photographs obtained by the reconnaissance commands and processed by the photographic staff, and also by information from other branches of intelligence.

The flow of requests from the 'customers' stopped at the Joint Photographic Reconnaissance Committee (JPRC), a sub-committee of the Joint Intelligence Committee (JIC) and answerable to the British Chiefs of Staff. JPRC was composed of two of everything: two Army, two Naval, two RAF and two US officers under the chairmanship of an American colonel. Their function was to sift the requirements by ascertaining if a target had already been covered and if so when, and assess the possible danger attached to a mission.

Requests then continued on their way to the Technical Control Office at Medmenham headed by Wing Commander Douglas Kendall with representatives of the Royal Navy (Commander MacDougal), the British Army (Lieutenant-Colonel Norman Falcon), the USAAF (Lieutenant-Colonel W. O'Connor) and Squadron Leader Paul Lamboit, the Senior Photographic Officer. TCO was responsible for all the operations at Medmenham and would allocate priorities. Because of the efficiency with which TCO was directed, a 'by-pass' route for requirements came into existence avoiding the intermediary of JPRC, which permitted certain customers to approach Medmenham direct through the front door – a system which turned out to be extremely profitable.

In addition, elsewhere in the unit, routine reports from sorties as they arrived would be distributed both internally and externally according to the names on the distribution lists which varied according to the interests of the recipient.

On the PRU side, the sources from which the photographs were drawn consisted of all PRU stations under 106 Group (Benson), Bomber Command of which all squadrons were equipped for day and night photography, Coastal Command with cameras capable of oblique angle shots for reconnaissance and strike photographs, and Fighter Command with cine-camera guns for strike attack. The American part of JPRC turned to the US 325 Wing (Recce) which was the equivalent to 106 Group and controlled 7th Photo Group (Mount Farm).

*First Phase Reports*

From the moment the aircraft landed at base after the sortie, the films were seized by the photographic staff and rushed to the

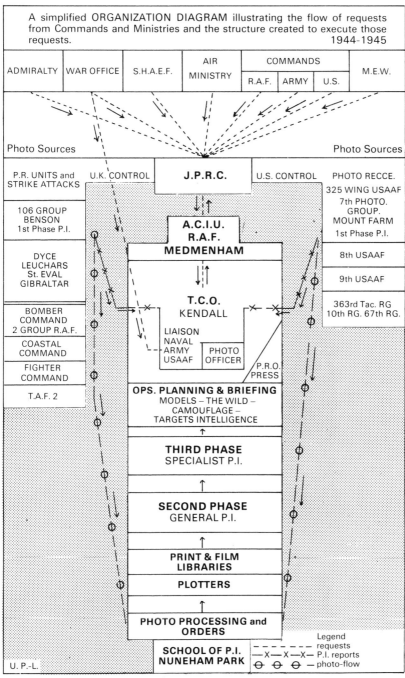

A simplified ORGANIZATION DIAGRAM illustrating the flow of requests from Commands and Ministries and the structure created to execute those requests. 1944-1945

| ADMIRALTY | WAR OFFICE | S.H.A.E.F. | AIR MINISTRY | COMMANDS | | | M.E.W. |
|---|---|---|---|---|---|---|---|
| | | | | R.A.F. | ARMY | U.S. | |

Photo Sources

Photo Sources

| P.R. UNITS and STRIKE ATTACKS | U.K. CONTROL | **J.P.R.C.** | U.S. CONTROL | PHOTO RECCE. |
|---|---|---|---|---|

| 106 GROUP BENSON 1st Phase P.I. | | | | 325 WING USAAF 7th PHOTO. GROUP. MOUNT FARM 1st Phase P.I. |

**A.C.I.U. R.A.F. MEDMENHAM**

| DYCE LEUCHARS St. EVAL GIBRALTAR | | | | 8th USAAF |
| | | | | 9th USAAF |

**T.C.O. KENDALL**

| BOMBER COMMAND 2 GROUP R.A.F. | | | | 363rd Tac. RG 10th RG. 67th RG. |

LIAISON
NAVAL
ARMY
USAAF — PHOTO OFFICER

P.R.O. PRESS

| COASTAL COMMAND |
| FIGHTER COMMAND |
| T.A.F. 2 |

**OPS. PLANNING & BRIEFING**
MODELS – THE WILD –
CAMOUFLAGE –
TARGETS INTELLIGENCE

**THIRD PHASE**
SPECIALIST P.I.

**SECOND PHASE**
GENERAL P.I.

**PRINT & FILM LIBRARIES**

**PLOTTERS**

**PHOTO PROCESSING and ORDERS**

**SCHOOL OF P.I. NUNEHAM PARK**

U. P.-L.

Legend
– – – – – requests
—X—X—X— P.I. reports
Ɵ Ɵ Ɵ — photo-flow

Organisation chart.

processing section. Possibly three PI officers would be on duty at the station, and would select suitable negatives for rush-printing orders, and not the entire film. The prints would be brought to them wet and from these an immediate interpretation report made.

The report would be of a tactical nature and was known as the 'Form White' distributed by teleprinter to all interested parties. It was normally completed within two hours (sometimes an hour) of landing.

First Phase interpreters had to be very experienced and capable of making split second decisions. 'Waddy' (Flight Lieutenant P.S. Waddington), at one stage a first phase interpretation officer, told me recently that sometimes a report would be made direct from the negative with the help of the pilot. 'A twenty minute job it might be,' he said. 'You had to know your area well whether it happened to be Bergen or Stavanger, or airfields anywhere in Norway, or maybe targets in the Baltic countries, and then at a glance you had to make the initial report. There might be twenty aircraft on an airfield and if the photographs were sufficiently good, you would have to identify the individual types. The same went for shipping; you might have spotted the *Tirpitz* or a battle-cruiser or a convoy, and the details had to be included in the initial teleprinter thing (the Form White) to be despatched immediately to the Admiralty. It was not only the interpreters who had to be good, but a lot depended on the information which the pilots were able to give us and which speeded things up.'

Two routine sets of prints of the complete film were sent off, one to Medmenham with the negatives that would be filed and indexed, and the other to Nuneham Park (Medmenham's satellite) arriving within three or four hours of the aircraft landing. The photographic officers were responsible for seeing that all internal requests for prints, enlargements, mosaics, duplicate negatives, reproductions of target maps and illustrations, photostats, lithographs and rota prints were filled. There are a great number of differing opinions regarding the exact totals of film and print production, but it is probably somewhere in the region of fifteen and a half million by 1945.

As soon as the prints had arrived at Medmenham, the plotters took possession of them and set to work to outline on maps the area covered by each photograph. This was known as the 'Plot', and the part of the map on which the plot was drawn would then be cut out and mounted onto card to become the 'master plot' from which

TCO (Technical Control Office): Wing Commander Douglas Kendall, Squadron Leader Paul Lamboit, Lieutenant-Colonel W. O'Connor.

Second Phase Section.

copies were made for distribution.

The plotters were a mixture of WAAF officers and airwomen with one RAF officer in charge, and as the war developed they became more and more overworked. The arrival of the US plotters finally alleviated the situation somewhat. An experienced plotter could, on average, plot a 500 frame sortie in five hours, and someone made a record of 900 frames in three and a half hours – these times including a half hour for mounting.

*Second Phase Reports*

Detailed reports of activity found on all sorties received during the day were completed and despatched by Second Phase within twenty-four hours of leaving the plotters. Sorties remained in the section until all the reports had been finished, when they would be circulated to the next phase of interpretation for specialised study.

Dealing as they did with all photographic coverage entering the one section, and working a twenty-four hour shift, the second phase interpreters obtained an overall view of any activity considered important to other branches of intelligence. This would have been impossible if bits and pieces had been hived off to specialised sections at this stage.

The repertoire of these interpreters was remarkable as they had to show more than a nodding acquaintance with shipping, aircraft, or military installations – in fact every subject studied in the third phase of interpretation. As the war progressed a certain amount of specialisation in the form of area reporting became necessary: daily airfield, and railway reports and Rhine Valley reports for example. On one occasion the section was asked to submit a study of French châteaux which were thought to have been commandeered by the German High Command, and on another, an assessment of the width measurements of German and Dutch inland waterways was required.

All references regarding shipping movements, port facilities and U-boat pens were held in the section, and to give some idea of the volume of work, the number of prints examined in one week during August 1944 at the height of the flying bomb attack, rose to an all-time peak of 154,399 with a total of twenty-seven combat films examined.

*

The work of the Third Phase sections, the final stage in interpretation, dealt with specialised topics and were named after

The Press. Flight Lieutenant Howard Symmons and Flying Officer Clarence Woodburn.

the subject: Army, Navy, Aircraft and Aircraft Industry, Airfields, Bomb Damage, Industry, W/T and Radar, Camouflage and Decoys. What could be termed 'Supporting sections' consisted of Photogrammetry (with the Wild machine), Models and Target material, the Print Library, the Intelligence section and a Press and Public Relations section. Interpretation as well as other skills were employed in the Supporting sections and they drew information from Third Phase investigations. Behind closed doors was a very secret body with the code name of 'Topography'. Detailed accounts of the work of those sections only concerned with PI per se will be found in Chapter VII onwards.

The small Intelligence section held a library of all types of publications useful to the PI's, such as foreign trade and telephone directories, books on industrial processes, reference books such as *Jane's Fighting Ships*, and prisoner-of-war interrogation reports. The section was particularly useful in linking reports from the Ministry of Economic Warfare with those of CIU.

The Print Library with its sub-sections for maps, traces, and mosaics, was vital to the unit, because at one time or another, all sections would require previous photographs for comparison with the most recent. Flight Lieutenant George Holleyman who took over the Print Library during the winding-up period at the end of the war tells me that the system of supplying traces of plot outlines to be laid over relevant map sheets was extremely successful. The interpreter, together with library staff, would be able to find the reference number of any previous sortie, and the retrieval of prints from stock could be accomplished in a matter of minutes.

At the end of the winding-up period, it was found that the Print Library still held some seven million prints and eighty thousand sorties covering vast areas of the world. The map section alone held a quarter of a million map sheets all relating to war areas.

The importance of Press and Public Relations was fully realised, and the section was originally set up at Wembley to deal with requests from Air Ministry PROs and press officers. Flight Lieutenant Scott was appointed as head, later to be succeeded by Flight Lieutenant Symmons with Clarence Woodburn as art editor, when it was decided to produce a weekly magazine from RAF Medmenham to be known as *Evidence in Camera*. The account of the establishment of the magazine is curious, as it was really through the persistence of Group Captain Peter Stewart, the Commanding Officer, that it became viable.

Peter Stewart was fully aware that aircrews benefited greatly from seeing the results of their missions on photographs – reconnaissance pilots because they had time to study their targets, and bomber crews because they could appreciate to some degree their success in terms of damage seen. He decided to set up a magazine which could be left lying about the officers' mess of any RAF station or unit, and after six months of correspondence, the Treasury Department granted permission in August 1942.

The title *Evidence in Camera* was the inspiration of one of the members of the section. A different cover was designed each week by artists in the unit, and splendid cartoons by such well known cartoonists as Julian Phipps and John Langdon, would make a weekly appearance. It was a first-class professional effort with a fine selection of well-annotated illustrations, with good informative captions, and short feature articles, the whole being competently indexed. It ran to eight volumes ending in 1945.

# CHAPTER THREE

# Back to School

I imagine that most hopeful recruits in photographic interpretation experienced the same emotion that I had when faced with the prospect of attending the training course: that of tremendous enthusiasm and an almost fanatical desire to succeed, blended with a deep anxiety as to the outcome. For some of us older ones, it was more difficult to apply ourselves to such intense study of an unknown subject, having left all that behind us many years before, and possibly having to relinquish a professional career into the bargain.

The selection boards of the time have to be congratulated on their success in being able to recognise the type of individual likely to make the grade in what to them was a completely new branch of intelligence. An extraordinary combination of personalities resulted which few people could have foreseen as being capable of developing the ability to engage in the work, to submit to service life and regulations, and to show the required dedication and loyalty to their unit and to their colleagues. I am, of course speaking of us civilians in uniform, and the list of professions from which some of us came is perhaps significant: professors, dons, lecturers in archaeology, geology, botany, distinguished painters and sculptors, photogrammetrists, photographers, a famous movie star (Dirk Bogarde), and an equally famous ballet dancer (Freddie Ashton), town planners and writers. The younger members who had not had time to enter a profession found their feet remarkably quickly to become part of a team.

For my own part, after having been rescued from RAF Records Ruislip by Wing Commander Hemming, where I had served my time in the ranks as an Aircraftwoman 1 or 2, I was summoned to attend the third (I think) course at Paduoc House, Wembley. When they showed me round the premises I noticed those buckets still remaining to catch the drops from the bombed roof.

The introduction to the course was the initiation into the sphere of free flying birds with their entirely different concept of the world we live on. Familiar objects become unfamiliar when seen from above, because recognisable perspective is non-existent, and therefore the shape of every object or topographical feature had to be learned so that it could be recognised. The principle of stereoscopic viewing when applied to photography came next, when the three methods of producing a photographic illusion of objects 'in the round' or three-dimensionally, was explained: the first method by means of a twin-lens camera with the lenses lying horizontally with the distance separation comparable to that between human eyes; the second by means of utilising red and blue colour separation on the printed page, and then viewing through red and blue eye-pieces (in the early days this method was used for land survey, photographs being taken from some form of aerial platform).

The third method was by the single-lens camera in flight. The pilot flies over the area required to be photographed, having set his camera, which automatically exposes the film at calculated intervals, expressly to cause each frame to overlap its neighbour by 60%. The exposure would be made when the lens of the camera in space was pointing downward at an angle as near to the vertical as possible.

Let us suppose that a specific building was to be studied by the interpreter; two consecutive prints in numerical order according to the direction of flight were selected from the covering sortie and placed under the stereoscopic hand viewer with its two magnifiying lenses on the desk. (These were always known as 'stereos'.) The first suitable print would reveal an aspect of the building slightly left of centre, while the second exposure, because of the interval of time, would show the building from a view-point slightly right of centre. These two prints were known as 'Stereo pairs.'

Owing to the overlap, the interpreter was able to adjust the prints under the stereo so that each eye would be staring at the building from a different view-point and it was thus possible to 'fuse' both images in space corresponding to the three-dimensional effect we enjoy from normal vision.

Sometimes, when I was a small girl, a treasured box of glass slides would be brought out accompanied by a wooden viewer with two black eyepieces, and I would be allowed to put a slide into the viewer and stare through the eyepieces at a fairy-tale world of sparkling snow, high mountains and dark trees – then suddenly and breath-takingly, my mother and father were standing like real people and looking at me – not flat people as in an ordinary photograph. The slides had been taken during my parents' honeymoon in Switzerland.

That childish thrill was felt by everyone who, for the first time managed to shuffle a stereo pair of aerial photographs into the correct position in the viewer. It might have taken a little time, and you felt convinced that something was wrong with your eyes, and you strained the muscles and tried squinting and then magic! Shapes in plan were transformed into real-life ships or churches or bridges. You begged for more prints, and like the child with its new plaything, you spent a half-hour in a wonderland of discovery.

Technical terms had to be learnt: for example: 'sortie' which meant a photographic sortie flown over a specific area; 'cover' indicating that the target had been photographed; 'verticals' which were photographs taken of the ground from an angle as near vertical as possible; 'obliques' photographs taken from a non-vertical angle; and 'forward-facing obliques' which were photographs taken by two forward-facing cameras installed in the aircraft, and capable of producing 'stereo pairs' during an attack.

Even though I had (and have) no mathematical ability whatsoever, I just managed to get by where the scaling of photographs was concerned. Generally all that had to be done was to pull out a map sheet of the area covered by the photographs, make a note of its scale (1:25,000 for example), multiply that by the distance between two points measured on the map, and divide that total by the distance between the same two points seen on the photograph, and the answer is the scale of the photographs. It was then possible to arrive at the measurement, say, of the wingspan of an aeroplane in feet.

It used to take me a very long time to work out the scale, so long in fact, that when I finally reached Medmenham, someone suggested that I should use a slide rule. For those who cannot imagine a life independent of micro-technology, the pocket calculator had not then been invented. I can say with pride that it took nearly a week for me to be able to multiply and divide with the help of the slide rule, and I was so gratified that I wrote a *Child's Guide in the Use of the Slide Rule (Simplified version) with illustrations*, to make it easier for limited persons like myself. To my surprise, Professor Glyn Daniel, the distinguished archaeologist, confessed to me recently that Squadron Leader Wavell, head of the Radar section, was never able to teach him how to use a slide rule.

It was imperative not to place the pair of prints under the stereo in the reverse order according to the direction of flight, as a hill would appear concave and not convex. Once when Royalty came to visit the unit at Wembley, a flustered interpreter set down a stereo pair in the viewer to demonstrate the effect of 3-D, but in the wrong order. The Duke stared for a long time and then, raising his head exclaimed 'What an enormous crater!' to everybody's consternation. What they had expected to hear was 'What an enormous gas holder!'

Trying to puzzle out enemy activity from photographs was a never-ending excitement for me, and the process of collecting clues seen on the prints and then to be in the position to formulate an hypothesis was immensely satisfying, particularly as there was always the chance of a dramatic discovery.

Track activity was the biggest tell-tale of all, once the interpreter had reached the stage of being able to identify certain objects of military significance. We had to learn that disturbed areas of grass or soil would show up on the photographs, much lighter in tone than the surroundings, and those areas depressed by feet or vehicles or excavations deflected light back to the camera at a different angle, thus causing this phenomenon. Track activity was almost impossible to conceal, and troops on both sides, we were told, were constantly being warned of its importance.

The actual interpretation reports had to follow a strict format, and we were warned not to become lyrical. For example such phrases as 'there is activity to be seen on the main line between Paris and Versailles, and a plume of steam can be seen issuing from the locomotive' or 'a hedge can be seen running along the side of the road' were frowned on; in fact the word 'running' was ridiculous in any context. We were never to use the expression 'planes' under any condition as this was for the layman – 'aircraft' or 'aeroplane' were to be employed.

The basic requirements to be included in a report were the sortie number, date when the photographs were taken and the focal length of the lens and the area covered; the name and classification of each target, when it was last covered, and then a description noting any changes since the previous photographs and any activity, of a military or industrial nature.

During the course, trick questions were fired at us to assess our reasoning ability such as: were these photographs taken over Europe or the UK? Answer: Europe because the traffic is moving on the right. How would you know a dummy airfield from a genuine one? Answer: Because of lack of track activity and the unreal appearance of dummy aircraft suffering from exposure to the weather as well as hangars not built to scale. What are those white things in somebody's back garden? Answer: If on a Monday the weekly washing. In snow conditions how could you tell whether a machine shop which has no chimneys is being used or not? Answer: By the appearance of the roof, as heat would have caused the snow to thaw.

For some of us with an eye for design, shadows were a constant delight to observe, as well as being of great value in actual interpretation. Normally we were instructed to place the prints under the stereo so that shadows would fall towards the viewer, thereby making it easier to identify an object, but in some conditions where there was water or flat ground, the shadow would produce a perfect cut-out silhouette of the original, but, of course, upside down. In this case the prints would have to be reversed, with the shadows falling away from the viewer, giving a perfect representation of a sailing vessel, a naval unit showing the outline of masts, funnels, and gun positions, or radio masts or pylons. Artistically the shadows were beautiful – the tracery of trees in winter, the outlines of cathedrals, spired churches or suspension bridges gave me enormous pleasure. Apart from these moments of self-indulgence, the shadows served as an immediate check in the identification of an object seen from the vertical viewpoint.

Inevitably some quite funny clangers were dropped: large circles fairly close together might be reported as four-gun heavy batteries when in fact they were harmless sewage farms, and a trainee once identified small circular patterns in fields in the bocage country of northern France as light coastal batteries, instead of recognising them for what they were – the consequence of tethered cattle or goats busy with their grazing, and munching the pasture in circles. If one looked really closely it would be possible to see a small dot 'moving' on the circumference of the chewed area. Movement was always easy to identify, as the objects would appear to be 'floating' or blurred against a 'sharp' background.

Some of the more agriculturally minded of our colleagues insisted that it was possible, when the scale of the photographs became larger with the development of camera lenses, to sex cattle from aerial photographs, that is to say determine the difference between a bull and a cow. However, there was an important proviso regarding lighting; the photographs would have to be taken

Ship shadows.

WAAF officers' course at Loughborough L to R standing.
Constance Babington Smith and the author.

during the early morning or late evening sun.

When the school was established at Nuneham Park in 1941, the curriculum became more and more sophisticated in step with the development of PI at Medmenham, and the intake of students increased extremely rapidly, particularly when US intelligence officers joined forces in 1942.

As we advanced through the course, the number of subjects we were expected to identify became more and more alarming. Technicalities regarding all the subjects included in this book had to be studied, and by the time the test was almost on us, after three weeks, I think, I was in such a state of confusion and lack of confidence, that I was convinced that failure was to be my lot.

I passed the course, however, and was accepted at Medmenham, working for a short time in Second Phase and then moved on to the Airfield Section in Third Phase which I subsequently headed with the rank of flight officer. The names of the WAAF officer ranks were confusing although they corresponded with RAF officers. Assistant Section Officer equalled Pilot Officer, Section Officer = Flying Officer, Flight Officer = Flight Lieutenant; higher than that the women could not go at CIU. In other places WAAF officers rose to Squadron Officers, Wing Officers and Group Officers, and the Queen Bee must have been something else but as we were not concerned with all that rank, I am unable to remember.

A devastating thing happened to some of us at Medmenham in 1942 or thereabouts. The WAAF Administration, arrogantly despised by technical officers, made the fearsome discovery that certain WAAF officers had slipped through the net for transforming the newly commissioned into Officers and Gentlewomen with the result that seven of us of mixed rank were prised from our important and secret work to attend what we thought was a laughable course at Loughborough in order to make us presentable. Professor Dorothy Garrod, that eminent archaeologist, was one of our number (although she does not appear in the photograph shown opposite) and being rather older than the majority of us, we did our best to hide her away as she loathed being in uniform and was terrified.

We were not the only people who suffered, as our instructors in the art of behaving properly were junior to three of us who were flight officers, and the poor things used to cringe and blush every time we saluted *them*, which, according to orders, was on all possible occasions.

# CHAPTER FOUR

# The Magnificent Wild Machine

I remember in 1940 being shown round the Wembley premises at Paduoc House and being led to an enormous piece of machinery with an officer seated before it staring intently through something that looked like a stereo viewer attached to it. My guide said in an awed whisper, 'That's the Wild machine, pronounced Vilt. It makes plans and it's very important and secret.' From that moment I decided to put the thought of that complicated metal giant out of my head, as I thought it could not possibly be connected with my future job. Later on I was often to see its beautiful plans, but I always felt that the Wild and its servants were somehow sacrosanct and unapproachable. One generally had to obtain permission to visit them.

Not only was the work of the Wild operators required for practically every MOST SECRET or TOP SECRET operation, but methods of mass reproduction for up-to-date plans of cities and towns in the occupied territories and Germany had to be evolved, as speed of production was critical. The draughtsmen and women were their indispensable colleagues, and although the work of the Drawing Office might not have appeared so dramatic, it was of equal importance.

Skill in photographic interpretation was essential as Wild operators had to be able to identify features, whether of terrain or ports and their installations, shipping, military installations or industrial plants. Much of the success in obtaining intelligence from small-scale photographs was due to the Wild machine.

The name 'Wild' was the cause of constant amusement to the uninitiated visitors to the unit, even royalty; HM King George VI on his official visit to Wembley in 1940, was said to have remarked when passing a bundle of envelopes marked 'WILD PLANS': 'I trust they are not!'

The Wild machine was named after the Wild Company of Switzerland, manufacturers of high precision mapping instruments, their latest model then being the A-5 plotter. There

A-5 Wild Plotter and operator

were only two in the United Kingdom in 1940, one being in the possession of the Air Operating Company at Wembley subsequently taken over by Air Ministry, and the second owned by the British Ordnance Survey at Southampton.

How did the instrument work? Harry Williams, former flight lieutenant in the Wild section, explains: The concept involved was that diapositives (positive film) of consecutive pairs of aerial photographs were mounted in two 'cameras', each in principle resembling an aerial camera, and by means of mechanical adjustment, were designed to take up the condition of tilt, tip and azimuthal bearing at the moment of exposure. The images of these diapositives were carried from the 'cameras' through a highly sophisticated optical system to a binocular viewing eye-piece (similar in practice to our hand stereos) and was then seen as a three dimensional image in space or 'space model'. An optical 'floating mark' – a small black object – was superimposed over the 'space model' and controlled manually. It could be made to move in three dimensions by use of a foot pedal, tracing the outline of all ground details, and plotting contours of the terrain under observation. All these movements were transformed through a complicated gearing system to a moving pencil which reproduced them faithfully at the required scale onto a map sheet. The principle is similar to that used at the present day.

Before Air Ministry had time to turn covetous eyes towards the second A-5 machine, the old Central Library in Southampton where it was housed was destroyed during the raids in the late 1940s. Only the massive seven-foot high 'U' frame in which the instrument was suspended, and its equally heavy base plate and plotting table were salvaged.

It became impossible for the lone survivor now at Medmenham to process the enormous quantity of work within a prescribed time limit, and ways and means of acquiring new machines were investigated. True, neutral Switzerland was sympathetic to the needs of Britain, but how to get a Wild machine out of the country when surrounded by enemy territory was another matter.

Because of his family connections in Portugal, Douglas Kendall approached the owner of a mapping company in Lisbon, General Sir Norton de Mattos (Minister for War to the Portuguese Government during World War One, who had received a knighthood in recognition of his help to this country). Both the general in Portugal and the owner of the Swiss factory agreed to co-operate with HM's government in London.

The idea behind a remarkable undercover scheme, was to send bogus machinery from Portugal to Switzerland. This was to take the place of the general's A-5 plotter then in urgent need of servicing and repairs. Flight Lieutenant Harry Williams had a hand in the first stage of the plot, as he was directed to search out various engineering firms in England, each to construct parts of that complicated and little known instrument, to specified designs, and they were told it was extremely urgent. None of the firms knew what the completed machinery was to be, or had any idea of its function.

The parts were completed in excellent time, and delivered to an assembly point where the now salvaged and restored pieces of 'junk' from bombed Southampton were waiting. All the necessary components for the construction of a dummy A-5 were now complete, and were hung in the 'U' frame and its base. The dummy was falsely weighted and then crated and somehow transported to Lisbon and the expectant general.

The second stage of the scheme was to disguise the dummy so that it appeared to be the Portuguese A-5 requiring urgent servicing and repairs. A typical company crate was found for it, labels and directions pasted on, and it was despatched on its journey to Switzerland, helped along over the latter part by kindly Germans. A short time later the 'repaired' A-5 (now a brand new model) returned to Lisbon, and from there it was freighted to Gibraltar to be loaded onto HMS *Hood* for its final lap of the journey to England.

Two of the huge instruments were really not sufficient, particularly as a new model, the A-6, had been produced, and so the same difficulties arose again. This time a friend living in Sweden travelled to Switzerland and bought two A-6s, ostensibly for his business in Stockholm. There was no hitch as regards this part of the operation, but how were they to be conveyed to England?

The safe transport of the two machines was largely due to the courage and endurance of Squadron Leader Ramsay Mathews, the leader of the section at Medmenham. They flew him out to Sweden in a reconnaissance Mosquito, where he was faced with two enormous crates of machinery, leaving him with no alternative but to dismantle both A-6s and put the innumerable parts into a series of diplomatic bags to be loaded onto the Mosquito. By then the

Squadron Leader Ramsay Mathews working on maps and plans.

Plans of submarine pens reproduced with the Wild machine.

**Fig. 1.** *Perspective View, St. Nazaire*

Base of Dock

Water level not shown

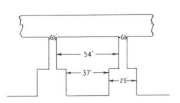

**Fig. 2.** *Sectional View*

*Fig. 1.* Measurements approximate. Perspective view of St. Nazaire pens.

*Fig. 2.* Scale. 1mm. = 2 feet. Sectional view of one pen at St. Nazaire. Vertical measurements approximate.

*Fig. 3.* Keroman. Perspective view of probable layout of S/M pens when completed.

squadron leader had become supernumerary, so he was stowed away in the bomb bay, empty of bombs and I presume with parts of A-6, where he sat wedged most uncomfortably but at least protected from the elements. Prowling enemy fighters attacked them over Skaggerak, and during the ensuing evasive action and unknown to the crew, the bomb doors opened and stayed open and he nearly froze to death. Harry Williams tells me, 'Big, strong, and fit character that he was, he survived', and now four Wild machines were safe in the United Kingdom.

It is difficult to select outstanding examples of the work produced by the Wild section, as the list is long; however, the town plan drawn of Berlin is one to be remembered. The only material held in the section to assist with this gigantic task consisted of an ancient Baedaker Guide and an out-of-date 1:25,000 scale map.

Suitable small-scale photographic cover was the first requirement, and members of the section spent many hours in the print library before the final selection was made. From these small-scale prints, eighty enlargements had to be made, bringing the scale to 1:12,000 and rectified. About two thousand contact prints had to be interpreted to obtain detailed information of the area, and as a very great number of the plans were required, the stylo method of mass production was later employed. The finished plan was enormous, measuring 10 feet by 8 feet, and was completed in three weeks. An added refinement was the incorporation of the central sector of Berlin at a larger scale.

Some of the questions put to the section seemed to the lay person impossible to answer. For example: what is the minimum turning circle expected of the *Tirpitz* when under attack? what is the volume of water contained in the Möhne reservoir over a specified period? From the Allied Airborne Unit which carried out an attack on a bridgehead on the River Orne: what is the height of the bridge? and we would like details of all its defences, and the heights of all adjacent buildings, trees and river banks. And from Bomber Command: what is the thickness of concrete on the roofs of the submarine shelters at Brest? and we would like the water depths at the entrances of the pens at specified times. People always went away satisfied.

# CHAPTER FIVE

# The Model Makers

The Model Section was another of the supporting sections with additional skill in photographic interpretation, and its history goes back to 1940, when the importance of model-making for briefing purposes was fully realised. An experimental section was set up under the Directorate of Camouflage at the Royal Aircraft Establishment (RAE) Farnborough. Model-making was quite unknown country for the authorities, and tentatively eight individuals under a flight lieutenant were recruited with a civilian of the RAE in charge of production. One of the eight was Geoffrey Deeley MBE FRBS, later at Medmenham to become squadron leader of the Model Section.

Air Ministry had no idea under what category the model makers should be included, as they were dealing with a new 'trade', so Geoffrey and his equally highly qualified colleagues were all grouped together under Group V Trade which earned them half-a-crown a day; thus the RAF was to benefit from the considerable skills of a group of people with quite exceptional talents in their own particular civilian professions, without the necessity of training them.

The small group of pioneers at Farnborough produced models of the submarine base at Calabria which was used for briefing the paratroops in the proposed raid, and also one of Pantelleria in 1940, but the project had to be abandoned. The Dortmund-Ems ship-lift was one of the subjects, and many models of enemy shipping were distributed. High-ranking officers came to admire, with the result that the work of the section was recognised and the section joined CIU in April 1941. They were first given temporary accommodation for a year in the basement of Danesfield House before being transferred to that elegant club at Henley-on-Thames, Phyllis Court, which had been taken over by the RAF originally for the WAAF officers' mess. I remember so well those beautiful surroundings during the war, with the wide lawns sloping towards the river's edge not far from the finishing line of the boat races in times of peace, and the shade of those magnificent trees. In 1942, the section rejoined Medmenham where they were permanently established in new workshops.

Flight Lieutenant Starkey, originally part of the civilian establishment at Farnborough, was put in charge with Geoffrey Deeley as his senior NCO who was promoted to warrant officer and finally offered a commission. The strength of the establishment rapidly grew to eleven RAF and WAAF officers and fifty-five RAF and WAAF other ranks before being joined by three US officers and thirty-nine enlisted men in 1943. There was never enough floor space and it seems a miracle that so many hundreds of models were produced on time for the various operations undertaken by the combined forces.

Two sculptors, eight artist painters, an engraver, an industrial designer, a medical illustrator, (famous names among them) were on the establishment, together with a leading silversmith, Leslie Durbin, who gained added prestige in 1943. He was given leave of absence for six months as he had been awarded, by King's command, the great honour of designing and fashioning the gold and silver work on the hilt and scabbard of the Sword of Honour to commemorate the defence of Stalingrad, which was personally presented to Stalin by the Prime Minister, Winston Churchill, at Tehran. According to Churchill's memoirs, he handed the splendid weapon to Marshal Stalin, who, raising it to his lips, kissed the scabbard. He passed it to Voroshilov who dropped it and it was then carried from the room by a Russian guard of honour.

Preparation of the model for the Combined Operations raid on the port of St Nazaire began eight to nine months before the actual attack on 27th to 28th March 1942. Four photographic sorties taken during this stage of the planning produced some perfect vertical prints as well as an oblique sortie. All during the period of construction, these were studied stereoscopically and the oblique prints gave information regarding elevation. Measurements based on all the individual buildings and quays were calculated, and detailed plans and sections were produced by the Wild Section for the construction of land form and topographical detail. The scale of the model made it possible to show alterations in ground levels and surface detail up to a height of four feet or more. Objects less than three feet were indicated by surface painting. The model was completed in October 1941 which gave time for the meticulous planning and briefing necessary for the success of the raid.

The section was involved in the planning of very many of the most famous operations such as those against the Bruneval radar station, Dieppe, the Vermork Heavy Water Plant in Norway, the *Tirpitz* by midget submarines, the famous dams of Möhne and Eder, the V-1 flying bomb sites, the V-2 rocket at Peenemünde and many industrial targets. The model-makers were stretched to the limit producing models for Operation Torch (the North African landings), in the autumn of 1942 as by then many of the skilled artists had been posted overseas. Later General Eisenhower, Supreme Commander of SHAEF, congratulated the team after they had produced bulk orders of hundreds of models for the planning of Operation Overlord, saying that their work represented a construction programme of great magnitude and that exacting time schedules were met; they might feel that theirs was a real contribution to the ultimate victory.

The finished models were sensational in their realism and beauty, some being very large with a base maybe of 8 feet by 4 feet. I remember seeing one which had been sent to Norfolk House in London which was for a time the headquarters of both Torch and for the preparations for our invasion of France in its early stages. This particular model must have been one of the first made of the Cherbourg Peninsula, and I found difficulty in dragging myself away from it – it was so spectacular.

How were they constructed and why? In simplest terms, these scale models were a three-dimensional conception of any selected area regarded as a target for operations by land, sea and air, and were used with conventional briefing. They fell principally into two categories; topographical models of large areas, or models of particular subjects such as ships, aircraft, railway rolling stock, buildings, port facilities and military installations.

The methods and materials used varied according to scale and the differing requirements of the 'customers' of the section. Scale, of course, was calculated in the usual manner from maps, charts, town plans or photogrammetric projection, and so a ground plan to the required scale was produced from a tracing in any photographic or pantographic process, with sufficient control points transferred to the model base.

Contours were then cut from card or board of appropriate thickness and fixed to the base, the whole effect looking rather like a terraced pyramid and providing the structure for the initial modelling of the land form. The vertical scale had to be two to four

A model of Kiel Harbour.

A model of Issy-les-Moulineaux aircraft factory.

times the horizontal scale, otherwise height would hardly be visible.

The next stage was to assemble the 'skin', consisting of correctly scaled and rectified vertical photographs, and then manipulate it while still wet, and stick it down on the structure, guided by the control points – an extremely ticklish job by the sound of it as there might have been distortion of the photographic image owing to circumferential radial or tilt errors. These errors would become enlarged on the 'skin' to scale with the rest and would need correction.

Help from various third phase sections could be relied on at this point, as their expertise was required for correct representation of the terrain, and the model-makers had to use their own skill in interpretation as well. Sometimes land forms and surface areas had to be re-plotted; this stage was one of the most difficult as whole sections of the 'skin' might have to be discarded or re-drawn. Man-made constructions would be added, such as embankments, excavations and defence works, and a colour applied over the entire area. Colour was a question of inspired guesswork of course, as they were dealing with monochrome photographs, but some indication could be obtained from surface texture.

All during this part of the construction, other members of the section had been toiling away modelling those features to be added – houses, churches, factory buildings, military installations, bridges, trees and hedges, for example, and it was now the moment to add them to the scene. They were made from cork-lino and wood and coloured as close to the original as possible. Finally the whole result was given a coat of matt finish to prevent 'shine' and annotations and symbols introduced.

Then the work had to be checked by a special group in the section, and checked again by members of Third Phase sections who had supplied information, and then it had to be photographed for the 'customer', using all the special lighting effects needed to suggest for example a moonlit or early morning scene.

Even as far back as 1942 it had been anticipated that the numbers of models required for the planners of Overlord would be very great, and therefore experiments in multiple copying were begun. By the time the section had been settled in their new workshops at Medmenham, production designs were well in hand.

What they did was to design a long-life plaster mould, cast from the original model, complete with all its three-dimensional additions, and from this, flexible plaster copies of PVC were

Model of the villa at Bruneval and to its right the Würzburg radio beam installation.

Model of lignite open-cast mine and processing factory. Ruhr area.

produced – each to be coloured and the annotations added.

Modifications had to be made to the mould as they found it could damage the original model, so various techniques were evolved and new materials tested. The results were wholly successful, and only the closest scrutiny could differentiate between original and copy. Altogether ninety-seven original models were produced for the planners of Overlord, and the sad part is I have been unable to trace any of them.

# CHAPTER SIX

# Drawing the Bow
## Briefing for Attacks

*Camouflage – Dummies – and Secret Missions – Decoy*
*Lighting Systems – Smokescreens*

To drop a bomb load accurately within a specified target area needed every navigational aid possible in the way of briefing material for air crews, and so it was that a target section was set up at Medmenham in 1941; photographic illustrations formed an integral part of the material contained in the target folders supplied to Bomber Command and later when the Americans joined the Allies, USAAF Commands also received copies of all the information.

The contents of these folders were very comprehensive as they held a target map showing the aiming points, two identical reproductions of mosaics (prints stuck down to make a photographic map) corresponding exactly with a 1:25,000 scale map of Germany or wherever. One of the mosaics would be annotated and carry a legend. There would be an information sheet with all the data about the target, flak defences, and the position of decoy sites. Often a large-scale portrait of the target alone might be included.

Each attacking aircraft would be supplied with one folder, and as some missions might consist of up to a thousand bomber aircraft, an enormous amount of material had to be processed. A very efficient organisation was required to cope with it all.

An Air Ministry department AI3(c)1 in London was master of the whole operation, taking charge of the intelligence for the information sheets, the editing and printing (not photographic) and all the distribution outside CIU, while our friends there in the target section handled the rest. Someone had to spend weary hours extracting suitable photographs from the print library, while others had the unenviable task of keeping all the information held in the section up-to-date; a job that every section at CIU had to face at one time or another. The time and mileage used up in communication with Air Ministry was phenomenal, with a continuous flow of two-way reports, and when work built up to breaking point, officers from the target section were posted up to AI3(c)1 to balance the load.

What caused the most botheration was the unexpected and sudden alterations of bombing priorities, when all work on one project would have to be dropped in favour of another. There might be a whole new group of targets added to the list in accordance with the decisions of standing committees such as in 1942 and 1943 when aircraft factories, submarine building yards and port areas became top priority, and again early in 1944, when attacks on the oil industry were extended by including minor oil plants and storage depots. Other objectives which had to be rushed through with little prior notice were the Möhne, Eder and Sorpe dams, the Peenemünde Research Establishment and the ball-bearing factories. Autumn 1944 saw a rise in priority of ordnance depots which meant over a hundred new objectives, and during the last month of 1944 and the first two months of 1945 nearly two hundred transportation targets were added. This reflected the high priority accorded to the attacks on the German railway system in general, and which resulted in the isolation of the industrial areas of the Ruhr Valley. In April 1945 emphasis was given to Armoured Heavy Vehicles (AHVs) and explosives factories.

A further upheaval occurred when the Americans began their daylight bombing missions because the target maps were designed for night viewing by the light in cockpits of Bomber Command's aircraft, and were quite impossible to read in daylight, so all had to be revised.

'Targets' followed the usual practice of working closely with interdependent sections such as decoys who were able to supply the latest news of the locality of decoy fire sites, and information about bomb damage assessment; industrial targets for example would be fed through to Air Ministry to help with their information sheets.

One of the RAF officers in Targets was Bertram Rota, the owner of an internationally famous bookshop in London specialising in rare manuscripts and first editions, who became a valued friend of mine until his death in 1966. He must have been a very dedicated officer, because, as a result of constantly nagging his senior officers, he was permitted to visit a number of bomber stations to find out for himself if pilots and navigators had any suggestions regarding the presentation of target folders. He spent many hours in ops rooms talking to station commanders and station intelligence officers; staying up often till four in the morning, talking with aircrews and learning from them what improvements they would like made; he even went on a training flight – a rare occurrence for

Target folder being made up.

The Dams' Raid briefing. The briefing was based almost entirely on the results of interpretation at CIU.

a desk-bound RAF officer.

During a conversation between aircrew, he overheard a new (to him) word in the jargon – the name 'Watermark maps' which meant nothing to him until it was explained and he realised its importance. Land marks, or prominent features as I have to call them in this context, took priority in visual navigational aids, and water was the most effective of them all. Because senior officers involved with targetry appeared to be ignorant of the fact, the presence of water was never given sufficient emphasis on maps and annotated mosaics, therefore the station intelligence officers themselves had managed to draw up what they called the 'Watermark Maps'. By sheer persistence, I imagine, Bertram managed to influence his superiors to have the omission rectified.

Loyalty Howard, a flight officer in the WAAF, although not working with Targets but in Night Photographic Section and bomb damage assessment, tells me that she had noticed that bombs destined for the Krupps Works at Essen were constantly being dropped about six miles from the target, and on examining the approaches of the aircraft, she realised that a certain 'watermark' seemed to have disappeared. On studying comparative sorties, it became clear to her that without any doubt Lake Baldersee had been drained, and the navigators had been using the bend of the river six miles away as their guide. As Bertram wrote: 'The centre of the target is less important than the means of getting to it.'

An early arrival among the American officers was Captain Elie Weeks, who joined us at Medmenham in 1943, and was later to become head of the French sub-section of Targets. In the United States, Elie had been assigned to the 1st Photographic Intelligence Detachment of the American Air Force School at Harrisburg, Pennsylvania, which gave him a head start over others of his countrymen posted to ACIU later. In a letter written to me recently, Elie made the interesting point that the system set up at Medmenham is now standard procedure in the American Air Force. I appreciate this comment at the end of his letter: 'As you know, the war made me a great admirer of the British'!

To give some idea of the speed with which the work was undertaken, Professor George Dury, who was in the French area sub-section, tells me that when a tactical target was to be attacked, they would rush to select the most recent and suitable photographs, order copies from the photographic section; go off for a bite to eat at lunchtime, and then return to prepare the annotations and the rest

Captain Elie Weeks USAAF in the Target Section.

Flight Lieutenants George Dury and Villers-David — Ground Intelligence.

of the tasks connected with their side of the operation. The finished product would be in the hands of Bomber Command for the night's attack.

Pressure must have been terrific when the Allied forces started moving across France in 1944/5, and the story goes that while General Patton might have run his troops off the edge of his remaining map sheet, ACIU's photographic maps always kept up with him.

Many RAF and WAAF officers were posted away from the unit for one reason or another, and four or five RAF officers from the Target section, including Bertram, found themselves at Air Ministry where in a round-about way I joined them later at AI3(c)1 in 1944. Although no longer on the strength of Medmenham our ties were still strong and visits frequent.

Bertram's secret tasks while at Air Ministry earned him a 'gong' from the Norwegian Government. The citation reads that the King Haakon Liberty Cross was awarded for outstanding services for Norway's cause in World War Two, and in his private papers, Bertram commented:

> I suppose the award is for having played some part in the organisation which collected and assessed information about enemy activities in Norway, using photographic reconnaissance, agents' reports, and the first class Intelligence Service of the Norwegian High Command in Britain, and our own Ministry of Economic Warfare. The ultimate purpose was target selection and the provision of operational material with which the air-crews carried out their attacks.

I feel that Flight Lieutenant C.B. Rota made more than a slight understatement regarding his 'outstanding services'.

### 'Topography'

Requests for topographical reports from planners of Combined Operations and Commando raids became so frequent that the Army Section at CIU to whom they were addressed, decided in 1942 that a sub-section should be formed under Captain Rowell.

The reports contained a general description of the terrain, the latest information regarding railway systems, roads, airfields, industries, ports and beaches, and overlay map traces was included, and accompanied by photographs and plans. Some of the areas were vast, and in fact the whole of southern France was investigated in detail, entailing a mammoth report of three hundred and seventy-three pages, twenty railway plans, and sixteen port plans.

The pressure of work was enormous, particularly for Operation Torch, and the run-up to Operation Overlord which had begun in 1942. Suddenly requests started to come through from the Air Ministry department Assistant Directorate Intelligence Photography (ADI(Ph)), asking for topographical reports for selected areas. The originator of the requests was unknown, as was the purpose, so not unnaturally they tended to get pushed to one side.

At this point, the head of AI2(c), the department of Air Ministry Intelligence, liaising between SOE and the RAF Stations, Group Captain Sofiano, enlightened the Army section that his department was the originator and hinted at more to come; but still nothing of the purpose was revealed. Probably because the Army decided it was too busy to co-operate, a sub-section of Second Phase was created under a senior officer, Flight Lieutenant Clive Rouse, and a file was opened for these special reports. Still the purpose remained a mystery, as they came under no category and carried no serial number. One thing was certain, however, they were MOST SECRET requests. Officially, the heavy security blanket was complete and utter.

Somehow Clive Rouse managed to work out a method of reporting for these mystery requests, and his section supplied fifty-seven reports from 1st September to 31st December 1942. The first stage in the procedure was for specific prints to be sent down from AI2(c) with the area to be reported on marked. Plots of photographs from different sorties covering the whole area would also be enclosed and the section was asked to select and report on further suitable sites in the area. By this time it must have become fairly obvious that aircraft were to fly over a pinpoint and drop something, or maybe pick something up.

A pinpoint and a two kilometre radius was the next essential, and if adequate cover were not available, it would be laid on. Very rarely the names of areas were mentioned, and if they were it was probably an error on the part of AI2(c).

From the 1st January 1943 to 8th May 1943, one hundred and thirty-four areas were investigated, and from 9th May 1943 to the end of the year, one hundred and sixty-three undertaken. The Royal Norwegian Forces required mosaics and topographical descriptions of very extensive areas of Norway, and the section was asked to search for a 1,000-yard square unobstructed specified area in Germany. It transpired that this information was needed to help with the planning of a rescue operation to free Wing Commander Douglas Bader – an operation that was never carried out.

There were only six interpreters on the job, and never more than two on duty following a shift system, which will give some idea of how the busy section worked. An officer known as the Ground Intelligence Liaison Officer, GILO, was always on duty in Second Phase, and he was there to collate items of ground reports related to photographic interpretation reports. When dealing with AI2(c) requests, the so-called topographical reports then became known as GILO Jobs, and for want of a better name Clive Rouse's section became the 'Topographical Section'.

The blanket secrecy imposed by AI2(c) lasted until 4th May 1943 when Clive managed to obtain an interview. All was revealed at last after about seven months of working in the dark. GILO must have been pleased and proud of their officer-in-charge, when a directive was received the next day telling them exactly what was required and the form of the report needed.

To begin with, landmarks seen from the ground and from the air were to be mentioned, and the targets selected had to be at a safe distance from towns, airfields and flak positions. Secondly, areas for Hudson landings (QH), Lysander landings (QL) and parachute drops (Q) had to conform to specified conditions which were listed.

For example'


*Hudson Landings:*   1000 yds x 1000 yds – free of obstruction –
(QH)   Suitable surface or three cleared strips 1000 yds x 300 yds at different angles.


*Lysander Landings:*   600 yds x 300 yds free from obstruction,
(QL)   suitable surface or room for 3 cleared strips 600 yds x 300 yds at different angles.


*Parachute Drops:*   500 to 600 yds – condition of surface not
(QY)   important – free of trees and large bushes – flying height 500 ft.

*Surface*:  Unsuitable if gradient more than 1 in 250. Freshly ploughed fields, harrowed or rolled land suitable. Growing crops over 9″ to 1 ft high such as wheat or oats unsuitable, and mown grass or hayfields suitable. During harvesting corn stooks or haycocks unsuitable.

*Obstructions*:  Fences, bushes, small mounds, ditches, banks, deep ruts on the side of cart tracks, telegraph poles, power line pylons. Anything not exceeding 6ft in height on the boundary, or outside the landing area within 300 yds need not be included, and beyond that limit only high obstructions were to be noted. These could be calculated from shadows, but previous cover might have to be studied.

These confusing instructions, apart from measurements and the list of obstructions, seem to me either obvious or ludicrous. For example, how could an interpreter, however experienced, be able to judge the height of a crop in inches? Moreover as Clive points out, it was almost impossible to determine what the condition of a surface might be (except where traces of damp were evident) or exactly what crops might be grown on it without additional long-term geological study and knowledge of farming methods at any one season.

Accuracy was vital within the scope of interpretation, because if any obstructions were omitted, the results might have spelt disaster. Clive Rouse was of the opinion that the interpreter needed a painstakingly research temperament with, if possible, some experience of the detailed interpretation of airfields, a knowledge of the countryside and agricultural methods combined with the usual PI faculty for minute observation well developed. A good working application in accurate scaling and grid co-ordinates was essential. Because of the excellence of his organising ability as head of his section, and the first class reports received by their 'customer' AI2(c), I am glad to say that Clive Rouse was awarded the MBE in recognition.

Although the actual purpose of the operations was not made clear until July 1943, Hudson and Lysander landing areas were for picking up Special Operations Executive (SOE) personnel, VIPs or refugees. Parachute drop areas were for SOEs and their supplies.

Lysander reception committees would be smaller than those necessary for parachute drops, and in fact an agile returning agent was able to see the aircraft down to the ground by himself at night. After placing his torches on the ground in the correct position for the recognition code, he would wait for the sound of the aircraft, exchange morse signals by means of his torch, light the recognition torches, and just before he clambered into the machine, collect them and his suitcase. The aircraft might be grounded for up to five minutes.

At the end of 1944 the work took on a new complexion because, owing to the advance of the Allied armies, the field of operations moved to Germany, and modifications of the reports became necessary. The new requests from AI2(c) were exclusively for parachute drops, and they involved pinpoint selection only, which to anyone not conversant with that type of interpretation might seem very easy. Someone worked out later that it took a single interpreter an average of ten to twelve hours per request, including chasing photographic cover of the area, annotating three sets of photographs, and allowing for time-lag in photographic orders to complete a single pinpoint. A former WAAF officer member of the team, Ann Sentance-Tapp, recalls that a request landed on her desk one day from the Group Captain Commanding RAF Station Medmenham. The request was entirely ex-curriculum: an old French lady was very ill in hospital, and desperately wanted news of her home near St Omer where her two sons still lived. Ann's report in very official language read:

### Farm Near St Omer

There is definite evidence that a normal agricultural routine is being carried on of which details are given below:

As far as can be seen on photographs, the house and farm buildings appear to be in good repair. The garden has been systematically cultivated and the hedges are well trimmed. Altogether, the property appears to be in excellent order. Although there have been bombing attacks on the neighbouring airfields at Fort Rouge and Longeness, there are no signs of any damage in the vicinity of the farm nor at the nearby village of St Martin-au-Laert. The following details from successive covers may be of interest as illustrating normal seasonal changes in the working of the farm:

3.6.42   Crops mainly cereal seen in early stages.

1.8.42   Noticeable growth seen in crops.

27.8.42   Harvesting well advanced, rows of corn stooks being visible in the fields.

16.9.42   The stooks have gone, and five ricks are now seen. What appear to be cattle are seen grazing in a meadow behind the farm.

8.2.43   Ricks removed. Numerous clamps show that root crops have been lifted. Manuring in progress.

5.4.43   Ploughing in progress.

Behind the stilted official language of the report lies a very human story, as the old French lady was able to leave the hospital in England after a little while when she had heard the news, and was said to have been well on the road to recovery. This first hand evidence, as from a neighbour having peered over the wall, of her sons being alive and well, and her home and property undamaged by bombs must have seemed like a message, not by aeroplane but from heaven.

## *Camouflage, Decoys, Dummies and Smoke Screens*

At the beginning of the war, the Germans showed little interest in camouflage, which was hardly surprising as they were in the strong position of being able to dictate terms in the struggle, and certainly did not anticipate bombs being dropped on the Fatherland or the occupied territories. However, after their failure in battering Britain to a standstill during the blitz, they realised that they might be in for a long war, so hurriedly applied themselves to routine camouflage of obvious targets such as airfields, military objectives, railways, canals, shipbuilding yards, industrial plants generally, or aircraft factories.

The use of smokescreens was another ingredient for concealment, to be followed subsequently by decoy sites for nearly every important target; some were to attract bombs during the day, and were designed to represent the layout of the real thing, with three-dimensional structures such as oil refineries and storage tanks, or foolish looking dummy aircraft parked on decoy airfields. Night decoys on the other hand consisted of structures, not to represent realistically objects in daytime, but to give the effect of burning buildings to draw night bombers away from their targets.

When CIU was established at Medmenham in 1941, it was decided that a separate section dealing purely with camouflage should be formed. Primarily its function was to act as an aid to bombing accuracy, and all camouflage information was passed through to the Target Section. Pilots were then briefed as to the exact position of their target which might have been rendered almost invisible.

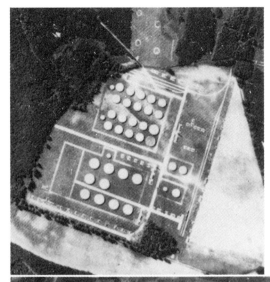

Dummy for the Hydro-Electric power plant at Politz. The site was very similar to the real target with dummy tanks, trains, roads, and laid out in the same rectangular pattern.

The head of the section was Flight Officer Molly 'Tommy' Thompson, an expert in the subject, lecturing regularly at the School of Interpretation held at Nuneham Park, and also in the position of being able to offer advice to our own British camouflage designers.

When the Germans began their programme of camouflage, it became obvious to the interpreters what they were trying to achieve, and Tommy, watching from the sky as it were, considered that the enemy approached the problem from a particularly unsophisticated point of view. For example, they would try and conceal an important factory in the middle of an industrial area, when it would have been more sensible to have left it alone. As it was, it stuck out like a sore thumb, which brings one back to a principle of camouflage in wartime; if it is there, it means that something of military or industrial importance is under it.

There is an explanation for the apparent ease with which the interpreters could see through camouflage, both literally and figuratively, while a pilot might have been deceived. Camouflage was primarily designed in colour to blend with the background, so that aircrew would be unlikely to identify the target as they flashed by overhead with no time to search for it.

Monochrome or black and white prints in front of the interpreters, meant that a range of neutral tone made it easier to define form, colour not being there to distract the eye, and also there was time for examination. If we had been faced with colour prints in those days, it might have been almost as difficult for us as for the pilot to find the target. One can conclude that camouflage was a failure from the point of view of the Germans if our PI's could identify the target, and a success if our pilots were deceived.

The main guides by which camouflage could be detected were from tonal dissimilarity caused by differences in the surface of any material used, even though it might have been indistinguishable in reality because of good matching colours. Shadows and vague outlines would always show through netting, and anyway the structure or framework itself might produce strange shadows after a period of being subjected to weather and ageing. By its nature, camouflage material would be frail with disruptive paint slapped on to break up an outline, and applied in large irregular patterns which would quickly wear away. Wind and snow would make short work of it causing netting to become transparent and then sag against the framework giving a sort of quilted effect.

Comparative sorties made life very easy, as if on previous photographs a factory might have been seen standing on a site in full view, the following photographs would show great activity with mounds of netting lying about, and efforts being made in disruptive painting and pebble-dashing. The pebble-dashing was used to break up a flat surface which in monotone would be fairly obvious when the whole tonal value altered with the light source.

Very elaborate structures were designed and built on top of existing camouflage to alter the whole outline, and, as Tommy described it: 'You could build lean-to's, or add roofs to make the thing look like a farm house with barns.' The camouflage designers would also go as far as designing dummy houses with gardens and trees on top of factory roofs with roads painted on, so that the effect was of a part of a housing estate.

An example of this method, according to an official report,[1] was the Fokker Aircraft Factory in Amsterdam. Netting had been stretched over the main buildings at a wide angle from roof to ground, so that their outlines were almost obliterated. They had erected the small dummy houses on the roofs, the painted roads, and the gardens and trees just like the adjacent suburban building estate. A small basin at the head of the canal had also been covered with netting and disruptively painted, and the open space round the flak position was filled with more dummy houses, trees, and gardens, while the guns themselves were perched on towers and given the same netting treatment. The writer of the report went on to comment, that the camouflage merged well with the surroundings, but the effect was lessened to some extent by the presence of a distinctive system of waterways, providing bomber crews with a perfect 'watermark', as the target people used to call it.

The designer, had he realised it, should have begun to camouflage the water surfaces, as it was possible to cover even canal-loops or aqueducts with netting. Great effort had gone into camouflaging the vital but vulnerable target of the Dortmund-Ems canal near Münster where it has twin aqueducts. The river valley below was partially netted by stretching it on a framework across the top of the valley and level with the canals.

Railway stations again were treated with very complex camouflage, Hamburg Dammtor being one of the many, where, as

[1] AP.3131A

Flight Officer 'Tommy' Thompson and the camouflage team.

Hamburg (Dammtor) railway station. Camouflage design of great complexity, the station roof attractively covered by trees and a road, while other trees have been 'planted' along genuine roads and a street island.

well as the usual dummy trees and bushes on the roof, others had been 'planted' all along a street island, and on the station platform which must have been pleasant for the passengers.

When I joined the section at Medmenham dealing with operational airfields, I was always fascinated to watch the lengths the Luftwaffe would go to disperse and conceal their aircraft. For example, at the end of immensely long taxi tracks leading to small housing estates, the aeroplanes would be accommodated in similar beautifully constructed little French, Belgian or Dutch suburban homes.

They were very obvious to us, for who wants wide concrete drives up to the front door? And why should they be so wide? And why should the little houses be just that much higher than their neighbours in the immediate vicinity? As if that were not sufficient clues for some, the shelter-houses could reveal even more, as doors and windows were painted on, somehow looking as if they could never open, and the whole front of the building was constructed to be able to slide open like a hangar door.

As for the airfield proper, general camouflage was effected by paint and which, because of being constantly exposed to weather and tear, faded rapidly. Some of the imitative painting was incredibly good when seen on photographs, and I would have thought totally invisible from a pilot's eye view. I remember having to glance more than once at a print of the small Dutch airfield at Texel which had no runway, before I could spot it.

Larger airfields with runways were much harder to conceal due to their enormous length. Even when camouflaged they were easy to detect, and constant traffic soon wore off the paint, and on the whole there was very little that could be done in the way of airfield camouflage of the more important bases. Recognisable features such as tarmac aprons, the perimeter boundary, hangars, fuelling points, taxi tracks winding away into the distance always remained visible to the interpreters.

Oil storage tanks were about the most conspicuous of all targets, and after the Germans had grasped the fact that disruptive paint made little difference, they decided to position the tanks in large groups and cover them with netting. Smaller groups might be placed inside a frame with a dummy roof.

For concealment of army targets, netting was widely used to cover gun pits, command posts and other military installations. A framework would be constructed to which the netting was fastened

fore and after treatment.
xel airfield camouflaged by
itative colour in order to
erge in with the surrounding
untryside.

and built up to the top of the pits, making a mound. Concrete casemates such as those for long-range coastal guns were very conspicuous, and would be draped with netting pegged out at a wide angle. Any constructional activity, always visible on photographs, was darkened.

The army storage depot at Pettin in Holland and sited among the dunes, was a very clever attempt at 'disappearing' something into the background. Each storage building was 'mounded' to simulate the actual dunes, and only the entrances and the dispersal arrangement of the units gave the whole show away.

Camouflage was not easy in the case of shipping, and particularly for a ship at sea because the outline and superstructure could never be concealed from the peering lens of the vertically fixed camera. Painting the deck was useless, but disruptive painting of the hull of a vessel might very well break up the outline sufficiently to confuse a reconnaissance pilot approaching for an oblique angle shot. A 'dazzle' design in disruptive painting was generally used.

Vessels in harbours, dry docks or shipbuilding yards could be effectively concealed by netting with or without framework, as it was possible to blur entire outlines completely, although superstructures were always visible to the interpreter. The mistakenly ingenious method of using cradles to cover the various stages of submarine building, proved instead a gift to the interpreters in assessing the date of completion.

A most interesting and elaborate experiment in naval camouflage took place during the period when the two battle-cruisers *Scharnhorst* and *Gneisenau*, with the heavy cruiser *Prinz Eugen* were lying up at Brest, prior to their dramatic escape through the Channel in February 1942.

Planning to mislead British Intelligence, the German authorities gave orders for the construction of a dummy *Prinz Eugen*, which was to remain behind while its colleagues slipped away in the darkness, accompanied by the genuine *Prinz Eugen*. The port was being photographed almost daily, and the interpreters watched each stage of the proceedings with incredulity.

The dummy was constructed from an old French cruiser, the *Gueydon*, with in addition two 250 foot vessels attached as a single unit at the stern to give the necessary length. A passable imitation of the German cruiser was achieved when seen from above, but in any event, joins in the hull were visible on a distant oblique

Effectively concealed. *Admiral Scheer* in Kiel Harbour.

The top photograph shows the *Admiral Scheer* on 7th April, 1945, covered with camouflage netting. The bottom photograph shows her capsized at the same place after the attack by RAF Bomber Command on the night of 9/10th April, 1945.

photograph, and would have given the show away from sea level.

Smoke screens were devised to protect important targets from day and night attack from the air, as well as from the eyes of inquisitive reconnaissance aircraft with their cameras, and as soon as German radar screens detected approaching enemy aircraft, a smoke screen would be raised. On the whole, it could be said that the screens, if successfully spread over a target, were a severe handicap to the Allied Air Forces, as well as presenting considerable nuisance value to the PIs who had to plot the smoke generators on maps, and make detailed plans of the layout.

However, the screens could sometimes be capricious, being very sensitive to weather conditions, and at the mercy of any change of wind. Furthermore, they were not easy to activate or synchronize. One PR pilot made no fewer than seven runs over Wilhelmshafen on one occasion; no smoke came up during the first two runs, on the third, three generators were in action, and by the seventh, only twenty were seen to be doing their job. The smoke was always white, so the experts decided that it must have been a 'water smoke', and described it succinctly, as 'The mist produced by a deliquescent substance emitted into the air, due to the condensation of water vapour round a nucleus of this substance.'[1]

Carbon smoke was not used, as the generator was likely to go up in flames, and so it was suspected that chlor-sulphonic acid was employed. Small though they were, the generators could be identified on photographs by the circular smoke marks visible round them after action, the marks looking rather like light-toned 'splashes' where the vegetation had been scorched.

To add to navigators' problems, it was discovered that the Germans were using decoy smoke screens as well as all their other decoys. When Kiel was attacked in March 1943, the smoke screen was raised, and at the same time another one was activated round Eckernforde to the north-west; later this was found to be a decoy, as there was no target of any significance, but there was a topographical resemblance between the two cities.

### Decoy Lighting Systems

It was easy enough to differentiate dummy structures from their originals on photographs, but how was it possible to identify and locate by day the structures designed to simulate burning buildings

[1] AP 3131A

during a bomb attack at night? The interpreters knew that something ought to show up, and it was due to Douglas Kendall that the mystery was solved.

He noticed some strange, unexplained structures in a perfectly empty field filled with bomb craters near Sotst in the eastern Ruhr, and took the sortie covering the area to Flight Lieutenant Geoffrey Dimbleby[1] then working in Second Phase.

'I remember Douglas bringing down some photographs and asking me what I made of them,' Geoff told me: 'There were rectangles which looked rather like buildings without roofs; with the walls in sections, then a gap, and then a section, and you might see a good two or three of these in the middle of a field somewhere. As I was new to Second Phase I had no suggestions to make. He said he thought it must be a decoy lighting system, and would I like to see if I could find any more. So I got busy, and managed to get together quite a collection with the result that the Decoy Section was formed with me in charge.'

The new team worked very closely with the older Camouflage Section, as well as with the Target Section who produced the target folders for briefing bomber aircrew. It was essential that all should be aware of the decoy fires surrounding a target, and Geoff's team also co-operated to a great extent with the interpreters in Night Photography who were able to locate the actual position of a fire-site from identifying the source of the decoy fires; and not only that, it was possible to determine from the day photographs what portion or portions of the system had been activated.

More and more decoy sites were constructed as the raids over Germany became heavier, and the target folders for briefing added a simplified map on which there would be a circular photo-montage portrait as it were of each site in relation to the target. These would be in the exact position of the pin-point. Cologne and the surrounding country had no fewer than seventeen decoy sites shared between seven towns.

Unfortunately not everyone appreciated these aids to accurate bombing and Professor Dimbleby tells me: 'When the crews used to come round on non-flying days, they were fascinated by this and it helped them. Then the heavy brigade came down on us like a ton of bricks; we were misleading the crews, they said, upsetting their morale by showing night photographs of these decoys with bombs

[1] Now Professor G.W. Dimbleby.

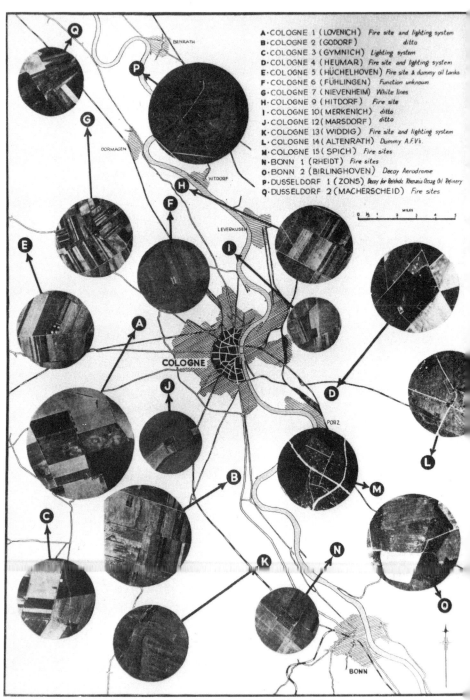

A · COLOGNE 1 ( LOVENICH ) *Fire site and lighting system*
B · COLOGNE 2 ( GODORF ) *ditto*
C · COLOGNE 3 ( GYMNICH ) *Lighting system*
D · COLOGNE 4 ( HEUMAR ) *Fire site and lighting system*
E · COLOGNE 5 ( HÜCHELHOVEN ) *Fire site & dummy oil tanks*
F · COLOGNE 6 ( FÜHLINGEN ) *Function unknown*
G · COLOGNE 7 ( NIEVENHEIM ) *White lines*
H · COLOGNE 9 ( HITDORF ) *Fire site*
I · COLOGNE 10 ( MERKENICH ) *ditto*
J · COLOGNE 12 ( MARSDORF ) *ditto*
K · COLOGNE 13 ( WIDDIG ) *Fire site and lighting system*
L · COLOGNE 14 ( ALTENRATH ) *Dummy A.F.V's*
M · COLOGNE 15 ( SPICH ) *Fire sites*
N · BONN 1 ( RHEIDT ) *Fire sites*
O · BONN 2 ( BIRLINGHOVEN ) *Decoy Aerodrome*
P · DUSSELDORF 1 ( ZONS ) *Decoy for Reinhold; Rhenania Ossag Oil Refinery*
Q · DUSSELDORF 2 ( MACHERSCHEID ) *Fire sites*

Target map for Cologne showing position of decoy sites.

flashing all around them – they sat on us, and it was made perfectly clear that we were not to do that sort of thing again. Actually we would let it lapse for about six months, and then try again. We were only able to produce three or four of these things before they'd suddenly realise it, and there was another rap.'

When the Pathfinder Force came into being, their task was to drop Target Indicator markers (TIs) for the benefit of the following bomber aircraft, and it was noticed by the decoy team shortly after the PF raids had started, that a different form of decoy structure had appeared; at a cursory glance all that they could see were rows of little white circles. Closer study showed an object on each one, which was interpreted as being some sort of launching device capable of sending up a rocket which, on descending, would simulate a TI flare. These rockets were very well thought out, as they had to appear exactly on time just after the actual marker had been dropped over the area. Furthermore, as the TIs were dropped according to a colour code, the German operators managed to change the colour of their own decoy flares in time.

Squadron Leader Dimbleby and Flight Lieutenant Samuel were given permission to visit decoy sites at first hand in July 1945, and they came back with a number of ground level photographs (now among the archives of the Royal Air Force Museum) showing the various methods of launching the flares, and the various different structures simulating factories burning, and even smoke screen generators set in rows round some decoy target. There is also a very interesting shot of what they thought might have been a former oil refinery with the fractionating column disguised to look like a church, and a dummy cooling tower with a central brick furnace, presumably to produce smoke to simulate steam.

Geoff Dimbleby remarked: 'When we checked the rocket apparatus on the ground, we discovered we were absolutely correct in our interpretation. The objects which we had seen on the photographs were little platforms, with a rocket motor fixed on each. On the top of this, they had a huge sort of Roman candle which was shot up to a height of something like 3,000 feet, I suppose – then it would burst and down would come the flares. We let some of these candles off in one of the quarries, and they were quite impressive, I must say.'

I remember Geoff telling me that once, when the team was interpreting a sortie flown over NE Holland, they saw numbers of small, staring-white blocks in triangular patterns, looking exactly

Former oil refinery converted into a dummy church.

like decoy sites, but it was impossible to make out what they were, and they were not reported as such. If they had received ground information that those peculiar white objects were, in fact, prisoner-of-war camps, their reaction would have been entirely different, and the authorities would have been notified immediately. Fortunately nothing was dropped on them, but, as Professor Dimbleby pointed out: 'It goes to prove, what should have been obvious to everyone, that photographic interpretation had its limitations in obtaining intelligence. We were in the extraordinary position of being treated like dangerous lunatics to be locked away if we were unable to come up with the required answer, without even having the means of obtaining it.'

If the German authorities had realised how much we knew about their methods of camouflage, and how we were able to watch every stage of the process, they might well have given it up as hopeless quite early on; except perhaps, when relating to dazzle-painted ships at sea, seeking concealment from others.

# CHAPTER SEVEN

# The Might of the German Navy and the Surveillance

In late 1940 Michael Spender (brother of Stephen and Humphrey Spender) became the first specialised Naval interpreter at Wembley, his skill leading from his pre-war expertise in photogrammetry, and the operation of the Wild machine. He was fortunate to be able to profit from the knowledge and experience in Intelligence of Lieutenant-Commander N.E. Denning, of Naval Intelligence Department (NID), who as Liaison Officer spent a considerable time at Wembley working with Michael. Gradually the value of these efforts began to be recognised, and a Naval section proper was established. Officers of the RN, RNVR, and WRNS did not appear on the strength until after CIU made its appearance at Medmenham, when there were about an equal number of RAF and WAAF officers.

One of the primary tasks of the section was to keep watch over all German naval units, battleships, battle-cruisers and heavy and light cruisers, destroyers, and escort vessels of all types as well as submarines; a long list which was later to include the navies of Vichy France, Italy, as well as Spain and Portugal against mistaken identity, and as various countries were over-run by German armies more naval units fell to the Reich, from Norway, Denmark, Holland and a few from Belgium. In 1940, as we know, many interpreters were caught up in the feverish counting of converted barges awaiting the signal to carry German troops and arms across the Channel for Hitler's 'Sea Lion' invasion of this country.

The interpretation of German naval units, and martial objects connected with the sea, was not easy for those not conversant with the subject or the complicated terminology – particularly the latter, as it was vital to master it, so that the PI did not make a laughing stock of the section or the unit. For example, it had to be realised that there is no back or front in that very special language; no right or left, and all the terms from stem to stern had to be memorised, and all the innumerable items on deck or superstructure to be recognised from above by referring to silhouettes or plans. The bemused interpreter would have to identify all types of guns, gunnery control towers, searchlights, hangars, catapults and rangefinders, and also show adequate knowledge about torpedoes and depth charges, mines, mine sweepers, and mine laying. Finally a concise, accurate report was expected without any land-lubber expressions. Silhouettes (fitted in profile drawings of enemy ships) were there to be studied and dossiers were made up to include all the prominent features, such as armament, position of funnels, with a sketch of the unit in plan. Movements of vessels would naturally be recorded as well as details from previous sorties. In January 1942 the list of those naval units of the German Navy over which the interpreters at Medmenham had to watch was long: the battleship *Tirpitz*, battle-cruisers *Scharnhorst* and *Gneisenau*, heavy cruisers *Prinz Eugen*, *Admiral Hipper* and *Seydlitz*, pocket battleships *Admiral Scheer* and *Lützow*, light cruisers *Nürnberg*, *Leipzig*, and *Emden*, and a solitary aircraft carrier *Graf Zeppelin* which remained under construction.

Accurate measurements and detail were vital, and the interpreters were able to benefit from the information offered by British Naval Intelligence, as it was realised when they received information that the bow of the *Hipper* had been altered, thereby increasing her over-all length. From their own observations they were able to report the moment when the stern of the *Prinz Eugen* was cut away after being damaged by a torpedo.

As for light craft, there were five classes of destroyers including the new Elbing class which helped to cause some bad feeling at Medmenham. It was a strange little story told to me by David Brachi, a flight lieutenant in the section.

David, who was one of the most experienced PIs in the whole of CIU, spotted for the first time, this new class of small destroyer, only 330 feet over-all, as compared with the two largest classes of 410 feet over-all. His correct assessment of the armament was that the vessel carried four light 4.1 inch guns, of which two were mounted aft, one forward, and the fourth between the two funnels, as well as four light flak guns and six torpedo tubes. The Medmenham plan and silhouette accompanied his report which was directed to the Admiralty.

Their Lordships reacted with vigour. They stated that it was not possible to mount a gun between the funnels, as that had been tested in World War One and found to be unworkable, and nothing would convince them to the contrary. The point was, as David

*Admiral Hipper* in dry dock at Brest. A magnificent low oblique taken early in 1941.

assured me, in the case of the Elbing class, it not only could but did work, as it could be trained on the beam – apart from the fact that to him, as the interpreter, it was clearly visible. He was invited to issue a further report to amend the original, but was brave enough (dare I say it) to stick to his guns and insist that his interpretation was based on photographic evidence. 'I told them I was not free to change it to suit their views, as to do so would undermine the integrity of photographic interpretation.' In any event, photographs taken by a Frenchman at sea level proved his point.

There were three classes of torpedo boats, three classes of minesweepers, E boats and R boats, six classes of submarines, depot ships, escort vessels, the famous *Sperrbrecher* (of which more later) and Q-ships which were anti-submarine ships camouflaged to look like merchantmen, and many others. When I was a small girl, I remember being taken to see a captured Q ship of World War One, and becoming very excited when all sorts of things were whipped away revealing enormous guns, and the grown-ups were muttering about the unsporting behaviour of the Germans.

Merchant ships were considerably more difficult to identify, as there was little Naval Intelligence to consult, but they were divided into five main classes; liners or large passenger-carrying ships, cargo liners which were fast and designed for the cargo they carried, and might have accommodation for a few passengers; tramps designed purely for cargo, coasters for coastwise traffic and short sea crossings, and incidentally a majority had their engines aft like tankers, with the funnel on the poop; there would be no derricks or hatches.

As if it were not enough for the interpreters to memorise all these points, they had to know the difference between ports and harbours, and all the odd items found in them with which to become familiar, for example different types of dry and floating docks, basins tidal and non tidal, jetties, moles, quays and dredgers. The latter were a source of great amusement since they were described as self-propelling or dumb, self-hopping or non-hopping, and could be divided into digging or sucking dredgers, not to mention the floating sheerlegs and the Stickerhorn unit.

Shipbuilding yards were often located on the mouths of rivers or estuaries, and a thorough knowledge of the layout and observation of the smallest detail was extremely important. For example, when a hull was completed, the slip would be greased (visible on photographs) and the chocks removed so that it could slide down into the water. The time needed to complete naval vessels could accurately be calculated from watching each stage of construction, from the laying down of the keel and the keel plates on the slip to the work on the hull; the midship portion being built first, and then extended fore and aft when the bulk-heads would become clearly visible on good large-scale photographs. The deck plating was left until the last. When nearly ready for launching, the vessel would look like a hull with very little superstructure, and after the launching she would be towed to the fitting-out basin when engines, boilers, armament and other parts of the ship would be added. It was the task of the interpreters to classify any new types and record their characteristics.

*The U-Boats*

The study of U-boat building by the interpreters has been widely praised for its imaginative and perceptive forecasts of the time required for completion, and this by continuous and devoted watch over individual U-boats from start to finish of their construction. Quite extraordinarily brilliant interpretation led to an accurate estimation that eight months would be the normal period for completion, plus three months for fitting out.

Construction would be similar to those of other ships, and the first stage was the laying down of the long narrow keel, which because of its shape would immediately indicate the function of the future vessel. Then the midship portion was constructed from sections conveniently left lying about nearby. It was at this point that the Germans assisted the Naval Section by their decision that each U-boat under construction should be concealed by a camouflage cradle made of a light framework covered by planks and a net which could be removed to allow cranes to work on the hull at any point. This was very helpful, as it was then possible to judge from the position of the cradle what progress was going on underneath. What made it even easier was, that as the hull gradually extended, so did the cradle; a perfect yardstick for the interpreters, particularly when, in the advanced stage, the cradle placed over the conning towers had to be removed occasionally because of its height.

During 1942, the production rate would have been approximately five submarines a week, varying from 1,000 tons at

Flight Lieutenant David
Brachi working on a U-boat
construction chart

U-boat pens under
construction at Bordeaux.
23rd September 1944.

Bremen to 250 tons to 300 tons at Hamburg, and these high figures continued throughout 1943. By February 1944 however the situation suddenly altered completely causing a lot of head-scratching in Admiralty circles because, from a total of 271 hulls under construction in June 1943, the number had declined to 168, and no new hulls were apparent. However David Brachi and his team found little difficulty in solving the puzzle.

In April 1944 at Danzig, a patch of debris floating about near a submarine close to the slips which had marks of oil and grease on it, indicated that she had just been launched, and when a previous sortie was studied, those same slips had been empty only six weeks before. Therefore the whole process of laying down the keel and assembling the sections had taken only six weeks to accomplish, but as it transpired another six weeks was required for fitting out. Prefabrication it was – a word not very generally known in those days, and certainly not when applied to naval shipping.

Two conical bow and stern sections were first seen under construction at Kiel on looking back over a sortie flown on 15th March 1944, and at Hamburg two odd-looking structures were spotted which were correctly identified as frames or templates for conical and stern sections. Later, similar cylindrical sections were seen at Kiel and Rensburg yards where their measurements were calculated as being 18 feet in diameter by 26 feet in length overall, scale being determined by the height of the crossbar of a nearby crane and which was obtained from its shadow.

There is a most interesting photograph (without an accompanying report) in the archives of the PRO. It had been taken from a ship as the outline of a porthole at close view can be seen, and some of these prefabricated sections are on the quayside of a harbour. Even with experience, it was sometimes difficult to visualize exactly what an unknown object would look like from ground or sea level, and this particular photograph showed a whole series of the sections positioned on railway flats possibly for transportation to shipyards. They have bands round them at intervals giving an effect of an armour-plated worm. The photograph, smuggled to England, must have been of considerable assistance in confirming the Naval Section's reports.

One prefabricated submarine, the type XX1, required ten sections. This vessel also known as the 'Electric Submarine' was designed for mass production, being entirely welded and prefabricated. It had an increased battery capacity and a very high underwater speed of sixteen knots; a range of 11,150 nautical miles, and a displacement of 1,612 to 1,819 tons.

Midget submarines were the latest acquisitions to the German Navy in 1944, and large numbers of 30 foot submarines were seen on photographs of Norderney and Borkum seaplane bases in the Frisian Islands in September and October of 1944. They appeared amongst sheds on the quays, and others were spotted in seaplane shelters; eighteen appeared at Borkum on 12th October, but it was noticed that all were withdrawn in November 1944. At Wilhelmshaven in December 1944 a number of these small submarines were identified on the roof of the airplane base building, while eighteen others were lined up on the quay. Larger 40-foot midgets made their first appearance on photographs at Ijmuiden, north of Haarlem, on 8th February 1945 when eight or more were seen alongside the quay.

Submarines, being the most important weapons in the sea war against Allied shipping, had to be protected when not away on their missions, and so the powerful Todt building organisation was given the contract for the construction of vast U-boat shelters in thirteen of the largest ports from Trondheim to Bordeaux. At Lorient, work was begun in 1941 and the very last submarine, *U-155*, left the shelter on 5th September 1944.

These massive structures could be said to be virtually bomb-proof (before the advent of Barnes Wallis's Tallboy bombs) being constructed of reinforced ferro-concrete. A detailed drawing received from a French 'warrant officer' indicated heavy lateral and longitudinal steel reinforced rods or railway line sections bedded into the solid concrete.

The most important feature in providing shelter from bombing, must of course be the roof, so calculations with the help of the Wild machine showed that the thickness of the concrete varied from about 11 feet 6 inches to a maximum of 23-feet or 7 metres. These figures were confirmed by ground reports.

At Brest, for example, the roof area over the whole block measured about 1,000 feet from northeast to southwest, and about 600 feet at the widest part. The height of the structure was about 55 feet to 60 feet, and the thickness of the roofing, originally 11 feet 6 inches, was increased later by two to three feet over most of the surface. It was later that concrete ribbing was laid, bringing the total thickness to 7 metres or 23 feet.

Flight Lieutenant Goodman of the Naval Section made a very

satisfactory deduction regarding the number of submarines lurking under their massive protection. If he could see from photographs the stern of a submarine projecting from the shelter, it indicated that three submarines instead of two as was previously calculated, were being accommodated and 'House Full' notices should have been fixed outside the other pens. He received congratulations from the Admiralty for providing vital information regarding U-boat battle order.

The first bombing attacks took place in January 1943, and were directed against St Nazaire and Lorient, resulting in the almost complete destruction of the towns while the shelters remained intact.

In September 1944 a mission was sent to France to study the effects of Barnes Wallis's heavy calibre bombs at first hand, in particular the submarine shelters at Brest. Flight Lieutenant W.A. (Bill) Seaby was a member of the team, and tells me that because of a three foot burster roof[1] having been constructed with an air cushion of equal depth over most of the roof, the majority of the medium calibre bombs failed to penetrate, and it was only the Tallboys of five tons with delayed fuses that could achieve this.

One of the bombs that Bill Seaby had interpreted from photographs in the Bomb Damage Section at Medmenham, had blown a thirty foot crater through the roof's surface with 'spalling' underneath, which resulted in an 'hourglass' perforation through the roof. U-boat personnel working away in, what they must have considered, conditions as safe as an underground shelter would have been severely shaken up, apart from the damage which had occurred in the interior.

The ACIU report was confirmed at the time by RE8, but of course the details of damage to walls and sections invisible on photographs could not be established until the mission was able to investigate at first hand. The plots of nine craters on the submarine pens and an account of an adjoining workshop being demolished were wholly accurate.

*Lorient ( Kéroman) U-Boat Base. The Sunflower Slips*
From the end of the thirteenth century, a small fishing harbour has existed at Kéroman near the point where the mouths of three-rivers join on the Atlantic coast of Brittany, and it has steadily gained in

---

[1] Constructed to make a bomb explode on top and not inside.

importance over the years as it expanded. During the reign of Louis XIV, ship-building yards were added to the port facilities as a result of the influence of Jean-Baptiste Colbert, one of the greatest statesmen France has produced. The shipyards were assigned to the French Navy, and many famous ships of the line were launched from Kéroman, the port of Lorient.

Inevitably the port and the shipyards developed with the demands of the wars in which France was involved, although the small fishing harbour still retained its identity.

Such a glittering prize was grasped with the greatest alacrity by the Germans in 1940, and one of the most important submarine bases in the world came into existence. U-boats from Lorient were able to operate within easy range of their quarries in the Atlantic, returning to base where facilities were available for careening and repairs, and where the vast reinforced concrete blocks constructed by the Todt organisation offered almost complete protection against all bombs except the *tremblement de terre* Tallboys, which despite their enormous weight, did comparatively little damage. Instead of the submarine base, the historic old town of Lorient was almost totally destroyed – one of the many great tragedies of the war.

My curiosity about the port was aroused originally when Clive Rouse, MBE, FSA, one of the senior officers in Second Phase recently showed me a reproduction of one of the aerial photographs of Kéroman taken in January 1943. Clive pointed out an extraordinary shape on the ground to the north of the Port du Pêche (fishing harbour) at the back of the concrete blocks of U-boat shelters.

The shape was slightly reminiscent of a flower; a large circular construction half enclosed by a light railway track forming the head, and the 'stem' consisting of a wide slipway leading into the narrow basin containing the fishing harbour. From the centre of the 'flower', similar to the points of a star, radiated six further slips; the terminals of the two on either side of the 'stem' where it joined the 'flower', entering what were obviously narrow repair shops.

The interpreters had noticed that in the very centre of the 'flower' was a turntable, and had deduced that a submarine would be taken to the head of the long basin, and from there transported via the 'stem' up to the centre turntable which would then direct it towards either of the two repair shops. I thought this a most ingenious idea.

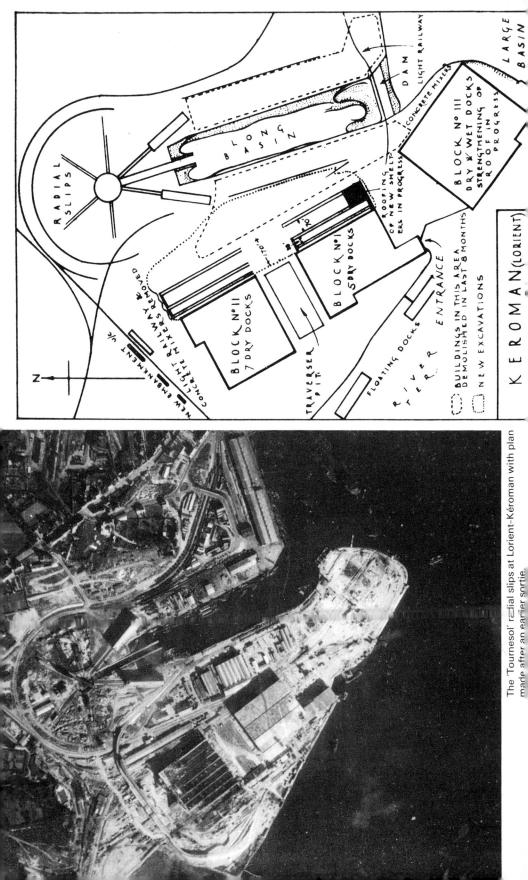

The 'Tournesol' radial slips at Lorient-Kéroman with plan made after an earlier sortie.

The plan (labelled **KEROMAN (LORIENT)**) shows:

- RADIAL SLIPS
- NEW EMBANKMENT CONCRETE MIXERS
- LIGHT RAILWAY RAILS REMOVED
- N
- BLOCK Nº II 7 DRY DOCKS
- BLOCK Nº I 5 DRY DOCKS
- TRAVERSER PIT
- 170 FT
- ROOFING OF NEW SHELTERS IN PROGRESS
- LONG BASIN
- DAM
- LIGHT RAILWAY
- CONCRETE MIXERS
- BLOCK Nº III DRY & WET DOCKS STRENGTHENING OF ROOF IN PROGRESS
- LARGE BASIN
- RIVER ENTRANCE
- FLOATING DOCKS
- BUILDINGS IN THIS AREA DEMOLISHED IN LAST 8 MONTHS
- NEW EXCAVATIONS

From the plan made by the Photogrammetry Section and the Wild machine, dated 11th December 1943, the *tournesol* (sunflower) construction of slipways and turntable is clearly outlined, and the position of the three concrete blocks and the floating docks, coincides almost exactly with a German sketch made during the war. Out of the three blocks, two, according to Medmenham, acted as dry docks whereas the third was a combination of wet and dry docks – the German sketch describing it as containing wet docks only.

Between two of the huge concrete blocks containing the dry docks, was a flat area which our interpreters had with remarkable insight named the 'traverser pit'. It was, in fact, a large articulated platform on rails, able to carry a submarine to the entrance of one of the pens or docks. The time taken to raise a submarine on to the platform and slide it into its repair pen took the men thirty-five minutes.

The two small repair shops in the *tournesol* area were of a remarkable design which was impossible for the interpreters to appreciate unless shadows were exactly right. They were known as 'Dome Bunkers' or '*Bunkers Cathédrale*'. The name arises from the shape of the roofs themselves which were vaulted, with narrow and high arches, covered with some sort of material which afforded them adequate protection against the smaller bombs.

Although the great concrete blocks have been retained by the French Navy (and who could take them away?) the 'sunflower' slips are now being used for careening trawlers, an occupation which for centuries has taken place at the same point.

Between 1941 and 1944, over 600 U-boats from 250 tons to 1,500 tons, as well as some Japanese cruiser submarines of 2,500 tons made use of the base. The last submarine to be careened was the *U-155* which left Kéroman on 5th September 1944 as I have mentioned before, thus putting to an end the activities of the *plus grand chantier de réparation de sous-marins de la guerre*.

*Blockade Runners*

One problem facing the Naval Section was that of recording the movements of those German vessels known as the Blockade Runners or Sperrbrecher. They were fast, heavily armed converted merchantmen spread widely across the oceans as far as Japan, and were able to run the blockade imposed by the Royal Navy to cut off supplies to the Reich, which had been trading armaments and aero-engines with Japan in exchange for raw materials.

Flight Lieutenant Sammy Sander, who tackled this job with his team, recalled that Squadron Leader Douglas Kendall approached him one day with the theory that individual merchantmen could be identified from aerial photographs; Sammy was left to cope with the problem as he thought best.

He decided to concentrate on the obvious course first, which was to study the largest ships to see if it were possible to find anything to identify a particular vessel. Something of the greatest importance was discovered, and that was the position of the AA guns. Should they have had standard armament of a certain shape, and should they have mounted the guns in a standard position, the team would have been 'completely scuppered' to use Sammy's words, for it would have been impossible to differentiate between sister ships. Fortunately, and this was unusual because of the Teutonic craze for order, there was always something just a little bit different.

Sammy and his team then evolved a card-index system which proved to be the basis of success. They were ordinary 6 x 4 cards, and were filed according to the length overall of the particular vessel. For example, the heading might have been '450ft, 6,250 tons, M18 (M= motor ship) *Himalaya*,' with a little sketch plan showing the position of the funnel. *Himalaya* was an up-to-date motor ship. Stereo pairs were stuck onto the cards if necessary when new or larger-scale sorties were flown, or if there were any changes in armament. 'For example, sometimes a ship would enter a dockyard with round emplacements, and reappear with additional square ones. That might have wrecked any chance of accurate identification had we not known of the possibility of its happening, as we held all the former details on the card.' Of course each photograph was accompanied by a full record of date, locality and the sortie number.

It was not long before these record cards showed their enormous value. The interpreters, closely watching the ports, identified a number of very fine merchant ships most of them fairly new and powerful appearing in the ports from St Nazaire to Bordeaux. They were duly 'checked in' on their cards, and to everyone's amazement were discovered to be following a weird series of movements. They would appear and then vanish, appear again and then vanish, and at last it struck someone that they must be the blockade runners.

These large merchantmen would load their cargoes in the French

Anneliese Essburger.

BLOCKADE RUNNERS:

Osorno.

Rio Grande.

Kauldi.

Scharlachberger.

ORE SHIPS.

Fidelitas.

Blockade Runners at Bordeaux

west coast ports, and then proceed to their destination in the Far East, and to begin with, during the winter of 1941 to 1942 they had considerable success in breaching the blockade set up by the Royal Navy. However, with the help of agents' reports, and ground level photographs which somehow found their way to the UK, the interpreters managed to calculate the total number of these ships and to discover many of their names.

*Himalaya* had an unfortunate and final experience. She was in the dockyard at Bordeaux on 15th November 1942; she then proceeded to the dockyard at Paullac on 23rd November 1942; she was next seen lying off Bassins North at Bordeaux, presumably laden, on 18th March 1943, and then spotted and photographed at sea escorted by several destroyers and torpedo boats, by Coastal Command aircraft. Having been spotted, the routine was broken and so the convoy returned, and the *Himalaya* was next seen lying off La Pallice (close to La Rochelle). She set off again, and was again spotted on 10th April 1943, and then retired to the safety of the Gironde where she gave up, eventually joining an ocean burial ground of scuttled vessels below Bordeaux when her final photograph, on 26th August 1944, showed her enveloped by smoke with the surrounding water covered by oil in company with other sinking ships.

Sammy Sander told me an amusing story about the Sperrbrecher *Rostock*. These powerful ships were converted merchantmen and acted as escort vessels. At Medmenham, the usual close watch was kept on this ship, and the interpreters were all fascinated to see, sometime after D-day, that she was being converted into a hospital ship at Brest. When this was completed, she then started moving up the Channel. Sammy takes up the story:

'We all knew about this so-called hospital ship, we knew it was a converted Sperrbrecher, and by then the authorities had received our reports. So they rushed out the Navy and they grabbed her. Everyone else was extremely angry because you do not go around grabbing hospital ships. However she wasn't a hospital ship because apart from what we had said about her, she had not been registered, so they took her into Plymouth. She was an elegant-looking ship covered in red crosses, and had approximately two thousand Luftwaffe personnel aboard her for a start; the intention was to smuggle them through the Channel to Germany where they would continue the attack against us. They finished up by being impounded instead.'

The Sperrbrecher (Blockade Runner) *Rostock* escorting the *Scharnhorst, Gneisenau* and *Prinz Eugen* (*above*) converted to a Hospital Ship (*below*).

The authorities, being understandably pleased with the interpreters, decided on a treat for Sammy and the Naval Officer who acted as liaison between ACIU and the Admiralty.

'We reported at Devonport to some bloke who organized these things. "Oh yes," he said, "you've come down to see over this hush-hush ship, haven't you? I've laid it on for tomorrow morning – report here at 9.00 hrs."

'We said, "Right you are, thank you very much, and can we go and see what she looks like? Where is she?" He then said, "What do you mean, where is she? She's there," pointing to a dock where HMS *King George V* was lying.

'We wandered down to the dock but couldn't see any sign of the *Rostock*, and returned to him saying that we were sorry to seem foolish, but we couldn't find her. The bloke exploded, "What do you mean you can't find her? She's staring you in the face." "But we're looking for the *Rostock*." "Good God," he said, "I've muddled you up – I've made a complete muck of it, you were to join the American Admirals visiting the *KGV* tomorrow." We said "We don't mind at all," and we had a terrific morning being entertained.'

They managed to see the *Rostock* in the afternoon, and discovered that every space was filled with wooden bunks. Sammy said there was still contention about her being a hospital ship and not a warship, but a photograph rescued from the wardroom showed a marvellous shot of the *Rostock* in battle dress escorting the *Scharnhorst* and *Gneisenau* and the *Prinz Eugen* – 'and then they pretended she was a hospital ship.'

### The Tirpitz Story and the Russian Connection

So much has already been written about the fortunes of the German Navy's major units – such as the *Bismarck*, sister ship of the *Tirpitz*, lost in the Atlantic after sinking HMS *Hood*; *Admiral Graf Spee* lost in the Battle of the River Plate; and the dramatic escape of *Scharnhorst* and *Gneisenau* from Brest through the Channel, that it seems unnecessary to include their history, even though PI was very much concerned with each event. However it is not so generally known that three separate yearly detachments of photographic reconnaissance and interpretation units were posted to Murmansk in northern Russia, from there to pursue, photograph and report the activities of the great battleship *Tirpitz* in the northern Norwegian waters, where she was out of range of aircraft flying from RAF bases in Scotland.

First about the formidable vessel herself. The keels of two large battleships, *Tirpitz* and *Bismarck*, were laid down in 1936, and to avoid the treaty conditions of the Washington Agreement which specified a maximum tonnage of 35,000, the Germans craftily arranged for a displacement of 42,000 tons. *Tirpitz* had an armament of eight 15″ and twelve 5.9″ guns, and for the benefit of the interpreters, the ship was broad in the beam, with a pointed bow and stern – her gun turrets were large and flat, and the gap abaft the funnel for the catapult athwartship, was very noticeable. Her length overall was 815 feet.

The presence of the *Tirpitz* was a constant menace to Allied shipping, and RAF reconnaissance aircraft were stretched to the limit in their endeavours to photograph the battleship from her first early days of fitting out and gunnery trials. So often when weather was bad she would disappear, and on one occasion in 1942 the Chiefs of Staff were more than relieved to learn of her re-discovery by a clever young pilot Flight Lieutenant Alfred Fane Peers Fane (naturally known as Fane Fane) who had previously worked as an interpreter at Bomber Command. He was killed later in the war. Fane's diary gives an endearing account, written as it was by an enthusiastic young man after discovering the elusive 'old row boat'. (I have retained the spelling mistakes.)

*23rd Jan 1942*
*Trip No 5 N/373*
*Trondheim and all fiords in area to find*
*battleship Turpitz reported to be there ( Successful)*
So that's what the flap is about! No wonder!!

Tommy and Freddie been out the previous days – as they were here already – but saw nothing.

Tommy asked me if I thought I could manage such a long trip so soon – said might as well do it now as any other day. Also my special training in photo interpretation and ship recognition might help. Admiralty intelligence was priority recce of same area again. Well they seem to be damn certain that the old 'Rowboat' is there. Their intelligence is usually damn good so determined to have a good look. S/C (set course) for Statlandet – climbed up to trails at 27000′. Flew on and on. Clouds cleared a bit near Norwegian coast – trails dropped sharply with temperature to 17000′.

Made land fall about 20 miles south of Statlandet. Weather hopeless for the job – so decided to fly north to Stat, and then turn for home. Damn (good) luck I did decide to do this – as when I got to Stat weather cleared and so I S/C for Trondheim. Photographed Trondheim and aerodromes – saw nothing in nearby fiords – so went north keeping good look out. Passing Aas fiord when I saw something like a ship hidden in the shadow in the far end – No, too big must be a small island – better make sure. By God it's a ship – it's *the* ship – rolled on to my side to have a good look and remember saying out loud –

'My God, I believe I've found it.'

Could not believe my eyes or my luck – Did three runs over it and next fiord and turned for home. Took Orlandet aerodrome on the way. Made Statlandet and S/C for home. Flew on *and* on! Came down thro. clouds on ETA. Clouds down to 600 ft over sea. Flew on and on! Began to get worried 20 minutes over due. Notice that there seemed to be a hell of a wind from the south so altered course 10° to port. Getting really worried – only 20 gallons left! ...

*Land!* Turned north and found it was an island – must be the Orkneys – yes there's a block ship – must be Scapa Flow, so turned south. Saw what looked like John O' Groats. (I had not had time to fly up and down local coast before I went on this trip and it was our first day up here). Just when I thought I was near Wick saw an aerodrome with runways – only had 10 gallons left – so did not argue but landed – only to find that it was Skitton – Wick's satalite. Only 4 miles from Wick – didn't know Wick *had* a satalite – so took off and landed at Wick – to find that they had seen me fly over with my wheels down while making a circuit of the satalite – felt a bloody fool – but with the bloody visibility and not knowing there were two aerodromes here – perhaps I may be forgiven.

Landed and told Tony I thought I'd found the old 'Rowboat' but could not believe it – *Flap*!!! Found that they were getting worried by being so late and sea rescue crew had been briefed!! Delay was obviously due to the 60 mph wind blowing. Hopped about on one foot then the other waiting for photos to be developed. When film was ready tore in to look at negatives. Maybe I'd missed the b- thing. NO! There it was – no doubt now it was the *Turpitz* all right. Rushed into the Ops room to report the news. *Flap.* I adore flaps, they always make me laugh. Group rang up, Coastal Command rang up – the Admiralty rang up. Poor Eve was up all night. Next morning signal of congrats from Butch (the CO).

Good old 'C' flight – we could not help laughing – a bit meanly – because the Mosquitos had been trying to get there for weeks and we get it in three days. Good old Spitfires!

Photos showed stereo pairs of Rowboat – complete cover of Trondheim – so my accuracy is getting much better but still wasting a lot of film. But I suppose it best to make certain than not get it at all.

Although *Tirpitz* was rarely in action, her movements were of major importance for the Admiralty, and thence for Medmenham, involving some of the most dramatic episodes of the war. The occasion of the ill-fated Convoy PQ 17 carrying war material to Russia via Iceland was one such, as even though the *Tirpitz* did not after all join in the affray, her invisible threat that she might be at sea was enough to cause the order for the convoy to be scattered on 4th July 1942 resulting in the destruction of the majority of the merchant ships by the Luftwaffe. *Tirpitz* was next photographed at Narvik Bogen Fjord on 17th July 1942 protected by booms. It had become obvious to the Chiefs of Staff that it was impossible to maintain routine reconnaissance over the elusive quarry.

As Fane's diary indicates, all during this period she had been watched by PR operating from Wick, way up north in Caithness and about eighteen miles from John O'Groats, and from Leuchars, just north of St Andrews. The difficulties were enormous – some of the sorties were flown direct to Norway, a distance of a thousand miles round trip, other aircraft put down in the Shetland Islands, while others refuelled at Vaenga I. Tucked away safely in the fjords, the ships were extraordinarily difficult to see from the air, as they enjoyed a perfect natural camouflage. They blended beautifully with a background of dark conifers, particularly under snow conditions, and could be almost invisible in the deep shadows cast by enormously high cliffs. The solution was the setting up of a PI and PR base in Russia itself, with British personnel working side by side with the Russians.

The base could not be regarded as a permanent affair owing to the immensely long Arctic winters, so it was planned to send RAF detachments for a certain period each year. They were to be stationed in the Kola inlet at the village of Grasnaya a few miles south of Vaenga I, and nearly 200 miles within the Arctic circle.

All personnel must have experienced searching qualms when they stared at their maps and realised where they had been posted. The north coast of Norway starts straightening out (as much as that serrated coast could be said to straighten out) around North Cape, and then turns south, as if it does not wish to intrude further into the Arctic circle. It joins the Russian frontier just west of Petsamo at Oscar II, and the Kola inlet lies to the east. The name of the town of Murmansk at the foot of the inlet might have been familiar to some of the group, but the thought of living in such a place far from home in a rigorous climate amongst a strange lot of foreigners speaking an extraordinary lingo must have been daunting.

Flight Lieutenant Harold Pusey, who was posted with the third and last detachment, calls it an enjoyable and unique experience, which in restrospect could be true, but one which must have been vilely uncomfortable at times. Intense cold, snow, ice and mud are not the easiest of companions. However, Naval staff at Polyarnoe at the head of the inlet went out of their way to be helpful and hospitable, as did their colleagues at Vaenga and Murmansk.

The first detachment, under Squadron Leader L.R. Wager, arrived on 23rd August 1942 with its establishment of pilots, photographic interpreters and photographic personnel, and with its brief to seek out *Tirpitz* and other units of the German Navy, and to report all movements and positions, as well as camouflage, booms, smoke screens, flak batteries, and flak ships. Oblique photographs were also requested of the entrances to the fjords. Three long-range reconnaissance Spitfires were flown out in September 1942 to join them. Film was processed on the spot, and a First Phase interpretation report would be signalled to the Admiralty.

*Tirpitz* was missing again when the detachment arrived, and was only located on 19th October 1942 when she was spotted moving south towards Trondheim where she was photographed with the *Admiral Scheer* on 29th October 1942 by Mosquitos, just as the winter darkness started to close in. The detachment was then ordered to return home, and having packed up all their equipment, they left behind three very important items for the Russians – no less than the three Spitfires.

Between October 1942 and August 1943, when the second detachment was posted to Vaenga, the interpreters had to rely on Russian photographs sent to Medmenham, mostly in the form of mosaics. Some high altitude obliques were of excellent quality although little use was made of stereoscopy. The correct overlap of the photographs was lacking owing to the practice of the Russian pilots of screaming through a dive and then pulling out at 10,000 feet, thus indulging in too high a speed for the camera to operate the exposures at the correct interval.

At the end of January 1943 the quarry was in her usual berth at Lo Fjord near Trondheim, which was later seen to be empty on 13th March 1943. She was next discovered at Alten Fjord (the twin of Kaa Fjord) in early May 1943.

The second RAF PI and PR detachment arrived at Grasnaya on 26th August 1943 and the brief given to Squadron Leader Fairhurst was to supply the intelligence required for the proposed midget

...ane's sortie of 23rd January
...942 illustrating the
...ormous difficulties faced by
...RU pilots in identifying
...rpitz in Norwegian waters.

...rpitz protected by booms
...he white dots) in Narvik-
...gen Fjord. 17th July 1942,
...fore the PR base was set up
...Vaenga in Russia.

...rpitz in Kaa Fjord. High
...lique taken from a Russian
...connaissance aircraft clearly
...ustrates the daring of those
...volved in the midget
...bmarine attack of 22nd
...eptember 1943.

ALTEN FJORD

TIRPITZ

KAA FJORD

submarine attack on the *Tirpitz* which took place on 22nd September 1943. Photographs showed that she had been severely damaged, and it was established later from other sources, that she had suffered serious underwater damage also, as a result of limpet mines, and was temporarily crippled.

By the end of September 1943 the wounded battleship had slipped away accompanied by the *Scharnhorst*, returning to her familiar berth three days later in Kaa Fjord.

The final sortie of the year was flown on 1st November, and as before the Spitfires were handed over to the Russians who were requested to supply regular sorties over Kaa Fjord as soon as the light permitted, sometime in February 1944. Only one of these sorties, on 1st February, was successful.

Flight Lieutenant Harold Pusey was posted with the third detachment to Russia, and was one of the two PIs on the establishment, the other being Lieutenant Newmark RNVR specialising in flak. They arrived at Grasnaya village in the beginning of March 1944 as a result of the Admiralty's plan to launch a Fleet Air Arm attack on the *Tirpitz*, a report having been received that she had left the Alten Fjord; in fact she had occupied the same berth in Kaa Fjord since the previous autumn.

In his report on 'PRU in North Russia' of November 1944,[1] Harold (by then squadron leader) stated that the primary requirement for the planned attack had to be the position of the *Tirpitz*, given, in all signals to the Admiralty, by six figure grid references for both bow and stern, on mosaics of Kaa and Lang Fjords covered by centimetre grids, which had been previously prepared and circulated. Full details of defences, camouflage and topography were included in the reports.

Harold Pusey has given an account of some of the worst moments at Vaenga; of the effect on aircrew personnel when Coastal Command decided to send tail-wheels as being the most obvious requirement, as they had been asked for them by the first detachment, and could not understand the necessity of oil tanks which were desperately needed:

Then there was trouble with the Spitfires which stood out all through the long bitter Arctic nights in the open. Ground crew heated the oil in drums over open fires, and poured it in smoking and revved up the

[1] Air 34/86.

engines immediately, but even so the oil chilled to vaseline in the wing tank. This tank, a few feet out from the cockpit in the starboard wing, had a small open air-vent on top of the wing in view of the pilot, to equalize air pressure in the tank.

During the early spring Arctic flights (although general icing gave no trouble) the semi-cold oil breathed off water vapour which, over the first hour or two of the flight, progressively froze solid around the inner walls of the vent till it finally sealed it, while all the time the pilot could watch what was happening. From then on the internal pressure steadily rose and the tank swelled and bulged, slowly tearing the rivets through the metal till finally it burst completely, and the oil slowly dropped out and slid back on the wing to hang like a swarm of bees before flipping off in lumps in the slip stream. A horrifying experience for the pilot being able to watch and gauge his own slow progress to disaster.

On 13th March 1944 the first full cover of the battleship was obtained by the detachment, and she was seen in her usual berth, along with a considerable amount of other shipping, including, significantly, two repair ships. Films and sets of prints were loaded on to a Catalina and reached ACIU in the incredibly short time of $26\frac{1}{2}$ hours from the moment of photography, via Leuchars and Benson.

Before the attack of 3rd April 1944 by aircraft from a naval force, including HMS carriers *Victorious* and *Furious*, when the *Tirpitz* was again immobilised, a very large number of British sorties were flown and a few Russian; but bad weather prevented further cover until 7th April when damage assessment was possible.

After further attacks on the *Tirpitz* were aborted owing to bad weather conditions, the RAF detachment received orders to prepare for their return to the UK in June 1944. Two Spitfires, tools, intelligence material, the photographic trailer with the remaining films, paper and chemicals were handed over to the Russians; the four pilots departed for home via Moscow and the Middle East on 12th June and after the briefing of the Russians by the British Naval Mission at Polyarnoe and by Harold Pusey regarding the continuation of sorties and interpretation reports to be sent to ACIU, the remainder of the detachment struck camp on 4th July 1944 for the journey back.

*Tirpitz* was again attacked on 15th September 1944 at Alten Fjord by twenty-eight Lancasters of Bomber Command accompanied by one reconnaissance Mosquito. Bomb damage was difficult to assess, and still the vessel appeared to be seaworthy – and then she disappeared to turn up once more in October at Tromsö having been towed there. The final coup de grâce was given on 12th November when she was hit by three 12,000 lb bombs during an attack by Lancasters. Within two hours of the raid, photographs were taken from a Mosquito from 17,000 feet showing the battleship capsized with the superstructure beneath the water.

*The Speed of Ships as Calculated from Vertical Photographs*

Interpretation officers of the Naval section became aware of a strange phenomenon seen on aerial photographs. They had noticed that any object, be it battleship or even insect (and probably they experimented with bits of wood on the Thames) when moving through water, left a wake consisting of a set of waves on either side of the object (let us now call it a ship) originating from the bow which, after all, is the first part of the ship to pierce the water.

These sets of waves would come together aft of the vessel in one continuous line at right angles to the direction in which the ship was moving. For reference, the peak of each wave was called the 'cusp'. It seemed to the investigators that the angle of the waves on either side of the bow as the water was being displaced, was constant, although the distance between the cusps might vary. The probability was therefore of a relationship between speed and the separation of the cusps, and a principle of physics must be involved.

It was important to know the speed of ships on occasions; for example should intelligence reveal that a formation of enemy naval units was on its way to intercept and destroy a convoy, it would be of prime importance to the Admiralty to know when it was likely to reach its destination.

Another advantage rising from this theory was the assessment of the speed of a ship during her trials if fortunate enough to be photographed by reconnaissance pilots.

Senior officers at Medmenham approached the Admiralty with their problem and experienced no useful reaction whatsoever – so they had to find the solution for themselves. Quite by chance, the very person who had the capability to undertake the investigation was working in the Naval Section all the while. Bryan Westwood, a young lieutenant in the RNVR who had spent a considerable time at sea in convoys before he joined the unit, was presented with the problem and began the research immediately.

The first step was to get in touch with the Department of Physics at Reading University, and ask them to search through their library for any information as to wave patterns and their relation to the speed of objects through water. What proved to be the answer was found in the papers of Lord Kelvin, eminent physicist of the nineteenth century.

Lord Kelvin postulated that any object passing through water sufficiently deep as not to be affected by the bottom, would set up the same angle within which the resulting wave pattern would be contained – whatever the speed and whatever the size of the body. In a ship, the angle on each side of the bow would be $19° 28'$.

Bryan applied this principle to the problem in hand, and submitted that the spacing of the cusps or peaks within that containing angle would increase in the ratio of the square of any increase in speed. Tests showed that this theory worked out precisely in practice, since to calculate the speed of the vessel, involved the taking of the square root from the photograph, and any inaccuracy in the measurement was of little account in arriving at the answer.

What would now be termed a hiccup then occurred. Kelvin specified that the wave patterns would not be reliable in shallow water, but for one reason or another had been unable to test his theory under suitable conditions, which in this case meant a reasonable depth of water. Bryan Westwood had managed to solve this problem and had proved the theory, but the Admiralty were not convinced for a very long time. 'The reason was that they would persist in testing it out with models in tanks, and indeed it wouldn't and couldn't work,' Bryan told me, and went on to say, 'The whole thing was dismissed until a young American officer saw the information and my drawings lying about and sent the whole lot to Washington. After what may have been months, they arrived back on my desk with a letter from the Admiralty saying, more or less "Look, the Americans have done this which you failed to do, and here is the way the US Fleet have worked it out. May we have your comments please." ' Bryan's comments were short and to the point.

At one stage in the investigation, Bryan wanted to back up the theory by photographing a British cruiser on its speed trials, and with great difficulty managed to get the RAF to co-operate. 'Somehow I managed to get my photographs which was enough to prove the theory correct, but still nobody would believe me. The

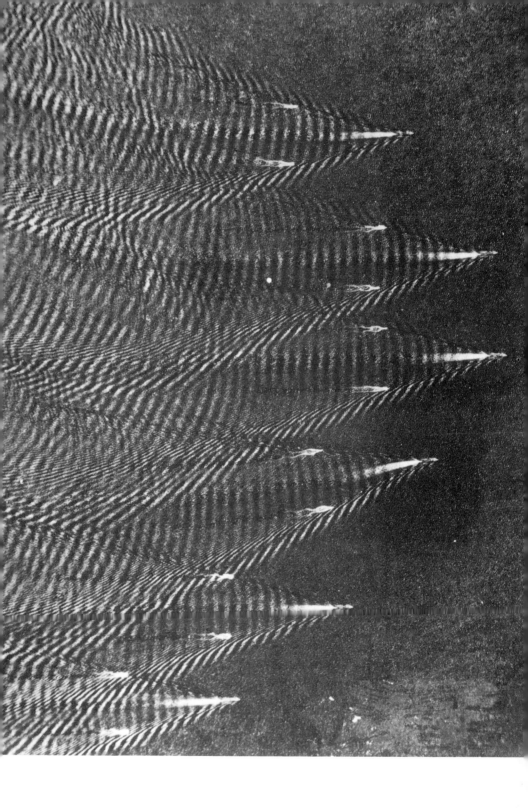

# SPEED OF SHIPS

...rmine the scale of the photograph. Flying
... may be used if there is no better data.
...he protractor on the photograph in the
...on indicated in the diagram below.
...ng an average of five to ten waves, meas-
...e wave spacing in feet. Determine the
...gle on which to make this measurement,
... first preference to the line astern (A),
... preference to the angle of 19° 28' (B)
...bsequent preferences to angles C, D, E,
..., J.
... the letter relating to the angle on which
...surement has been taken and against the
...onding column of the table read the speed
... ship in knots. Intermediate measurements
...les must be determined by inspection.
... depth of water on chart and see that it
...ficient to permit estimate of speed.

| KNOTS | SPACE BETWEEN WAVES IN FEET | | | | | | | | | KNOTS | Essential depth of water for reliable estimate. FATHOMS. |
| | A ASTERN. | B 19° 28' | C | D | E | F | G | H | J | | |
|---|---|---|---|---|---|---|---|---|---|---|---|
| 4 | 8 | 11 | 10 | 9 | 8 | 7 | 6 | 5 | 3½ | 4 | - |
| 5 | 12 | 17 | 16 | 14 | 13 | 11 | 9½ | 7½ | 5½ | 5 | - |
| 6 | 18 | 24 | 23 | 20 | 18 | 16 | 13 | 11 | 8 | 6 | - |
| 7 | 25 | 32 | 30 | 27 | 24 | 21 | 18 | 14 | 11 | 7 | - |
| 8 | 33 | 41 | 38 | 35 | 31 | 27 | 23 | 19 | 14 | 8 | 1 |
| 9 | 42 | 52 | 48 | 44 | 39 | 35 | 29 | 23 | 17 | 9 | - |
| 10 | 53 | 64 | 60 | 54 | 48 | 42 | 36 | 29 | 21 | 10 | 1½ |
| 11 | 65 | 77 | 72 | 65 | 58 | 51 | 43 | 34 | 26 | 11 | - |
| 12 | 78 | 92 | 86 | 78 | 70 | 60 | 51 | 41 | 31 | 12 | 2½ |
| 13 | 91 | 110 | 100 | 92 | 82 | 71 | 60 | 48 | 36 | 13 | - |
| 14 | 105 | 125 | 115 | 105 | 94 | 82 | 70 | 56 | 42 | 14 | 3¼ |
| 15 | 120 | 145 | 135 | 125 | 110 | 95 | 80 | 65 | 48 | 15 | 4 |
| 16 | 140 | 165 | 155 | 140 | 125 | 110 | 92 | 74 | 55 | 16 | 4½ |
| 17 | 155 | 185 | 175 | 160 | 140 | 125 | 105 | 83 | 62 | 17 | 5 |
| 18 | 170 | 210 | 195 | 175 | 160 | 135 | 115 | 93 | 69 | 18 | 5½ |
| 19 | 190 | 230 | 220 | 200 | 175 | 155 | 130 | 105 | 77 | 19 | 6 |
| 20 | 210 | 255 | 240 | 220 | 195 | 170 | 140 | 115 | 85 | 20 | 7¼ |
| 22 | 250 | 310 | 290 | 265 | 235 | 205 | 170 | 140 | 105 | 22 | 9 |
| 24 | - | 370 | 345 | 315 | 280 | 240 | 205 | 165 | 125 | 24 | 10½ |
| 26 | - | 435 | 410 | 370 | 330 | 285 | 240 | 195 | 145 | 26 | 12 |
| 28 | - | 505 | 475 | 430 | 380 | 330 | 280 | 225 | 170 | 28 | 14 |
| 30 | - | 580 | 545 | 495 | 440 | 380 | 320 | 260 | 195 | 30 | 16 |
| 32 | - | 660 | 620 | 560 | 500 | 435 | 370 | 295 | 220 | 32 | 18 |
| 34 | - | 745 | 700 | 630 | 565 | 490 | 415 | 330 | 250 | 34 | 20 |
| 36 | - | 830 | 780 | 705 | 630 | 545 | 460 | 370 | 275 | 36 | 22 |
| 38 | - | 920 | 865 | 785 | 700 | 605 | 515 | 410 | 305 | 38 | 24 |
| 40 | - | 1025 | 965 | 870 | 780 | 675 | 570 | 455 | 340 | 40 | - |

(Left) A vertical photograph of the wake made by German mine sweepers and their sweeps which demonstrates the principle involved in calculating the speed of ships and (above) the calculator designed for that purpose.

Americans, much more sensibly, tied a balloon to the stern of a destroyer with a camera attached to it which took the photographs of the ship on its speed trials which were very accurately recorded. The findings were that our theory was accurate to less than half a knot.'

When the theory had been finally accepted, all that was required of the interpreter when assessing speed was first to determine the scale of the photograph, and then with a specially designed protractor laid over the photograph, to calculate the distance between the cusps in feet (taking an average of five to ten waves). The answer would be found by referring to a table capable not only of producing the speed of the ship in knots, but the essential depth of the water in fathoms for a reliable estimate.

Now that the interpreters held the method of obtaining the information in their hands, two fortuitous and valuable events occurred. The first was included in a message Ultra received by Medmenham from Bletchley Park. The message was to the effect that *Bismarck* was due to go on her speed trials, and the locality was given. Photographic reconnaissance was laid on, excellent photographs obtained and the speed of the battleship was recorded as 31 knots.

The second event happened by chance when photographs were taken of a *Sperrbrecher*, one of the many which had been converted into minesweepers by the installation of powerful magnets in their bows enabling them to detonate harmlessly British magnetic mines. The photographs showed, not only the ripples made by the explosion, but the *Sperrbrecher* as well steaming away from it at a distance of about 400 yards. By measuring on successsive prints, it was possible to calculate the rate of travel outwards of the ripples from the point of the explosion, as well as the speed of the ship. The position of the *Sperrbrecher* in relation to the mine when it was detonated could be determined, and thus the effective magnetic field of the mine. Obviously from that time on, it was possible to sow the odd magnetic mine with a built-in delay so it would take the minesweeper by surprise when next sweeping the same channel.

A development of the theory took place later in the war, not from the angle of vertical photography, but from the view-point of the periscope of a submarine. Supposing that a submariner were given the order to fire a torpedo at, for example, an enemy naval unit, he would require the speed of the vessel as well as the range to make his calculations for the setting, and this could be achieved by measuring the distance between successive waves moving along the side of the ship.

Strangely enough, the Japanese had arrived at the same point in the research, as was discovered from captured documents.

# CHAPTER EIGHT

# Wehrmacht under the Stereo
# ... And Operational Planning

The tasks of the Army Photographic Interpretation Section (APIS), when established at Medmenham in 1941, were the continuation of those undertaken at Wembley, in particular the German defence measures which were beginning to be noticed on the photographs.

The basis of the work was the map sheet and dossier system whereby all coastal gun batteries as well as flak sites were plotted on master maps, and all details recorded for the dossiers. Within forty-eight hours of photographs being received, two reports giving general military and flak information would be prepared together with an up-dated flak overlay trace of the area for distribution to the originator of requests for information such as the War Office military intelligence (MI) departments and Air Intelligence at Air Ministry. Another extremely important task was to confirm or not any intelligence reports from other sources that might be submitted for query, and to distribute suitable information for use during interrogation.

By the autumn of 1941 the system began to creak owing to pressure of work, and therefore specific areas were allotted to individual interpreters whose job it was to deal with only one country or section of a country at a time. APIS also had to provide coastal mosaics for the benefit of army commands who by then had been allocated intelligence responsibility for each section of the enemy-held coast.

Early in 1942, the Combined Operations Forces came under the command of Admiral Mountbatten, and one of his first tasks was the capture on 27th February 1942 of the Bruneval radar beam station at Cap d'Antifer near Le Havre, the first Würzburg paraboloid radar installations to be identified. APIS shouldered the task of investigating every inch of the terrain surrounding the villa which was the headquarters of the radar complex and in the grounds of which the Würzburg had been installed.

All defences and topographical details for parachute dropping had to be reported by the section, and as Neil Simon, then Major, tells me. 'There were two valleys approaching the villa from the rear making it possible for a two-pronged attack. We did not report unidentified dark areas which might have proved to be any sort of low vegetation, and of course these turned out to be brambles which the soldiers had to hack their way through.'

One can imagine the thoughts of the soldiers at the time, which goes to show that with all the expertise in the world, interpreters could not be expected to work miracles.

The planning of every individual operation depended essentially on the aerial photographs obtained by the RAF, the APIS interpretation reports, and models supplied by Medmenham which in their turn included all the German defences. For the St Nazaire raid of 27th/28th March 1942 vital information regarding the defences of the port, in the shape of four heavy coastal batteries, was discovered by the section, and included in the model constructed for the briefing of the landing party.

In May 1942, part of APIS was hived off to form another section at GHQ Home Forces based at Norfolk House, St James' Square, London. Gradually the division of responsibility between the new APIS (GHQ) and APIS (CIU) became more clearly defined. GHQ was to concentrate on the German defences in preparation for our invasion of Europe, while CIU at Medmenham was to concern itself with the surveillance of the enemy artillery further inland, especially the location and strength of flak batteries. The accuracy in plotting these batteries was, as before, of vital importance for briefing air crews, and also led to MI10's flak maps being produced at Medmenham combining APIS records and other inte'''igence supplied from MI10.

A mammoth task faced APIS at Norfolk House, as all photographs taken within thirty miles of the coast from Den Helder to the Franco-Spanish border had to be examined in order to plot every military installation identified. To the everlasting credit of the army interpreters, 90% of all existing batteries were identified, the remaining 10% being largely mobile flak batteries. To make the task even more difficult, all the maps of the area had to be re-drawn because the existing ones were completely out of date, being based on a sixty-year-old French survey.

Not only the planning staff for the invasion of North-West mainland Europe were detached to Norfolk House, but also those for the Allied landings in North Africa – Operation Torch – with a number of the army interpreters from Medmenham among them.

The Dieppe raid, which was a prototype for Operation Overlord, took place on 19th August 1942 with over 6,000 British and Canadian troops. APIS and the model section, bomb damage and airfield sections, were stretched to the limit in supplying whatever information was asked of them, and the lessons learnt from the raid were of the greatest value.

The problem of moving tanks or other army motorised vehicles off the beaches was found to be extremely complex. Tanks became inextricably bogged down in gravel, with the result that a number of geologists were subsequently attached to the army planners and to APIS as intelligence officers. It was explained to me that a beach made up of pebbles of approximately the same size, is terrible stuff for army vehicles, particularly tanks, as they just grind to a halt, since similar size pebbles have a ball-bearing effect. What is essential is a hard surface consisting of gravels of different grades and varying sizes, and the only way to find out was to be given the opportunity to study them at first hand. Personnel were therefore sent off by submarine to collect samples.

Lessons regarding underwater obstacles were also learnt from Dieppe, and were applied to Overlord planning, as landing craft endeavouring to get to the beach encountered steel stakes and curved rails driven into the sand below the water line. Another unpleasant trap was discovered by the interpreters off one of the Normandy beaches. They had noticed that a large number of obstacles were being planted below the waterline, with curious objects attached to them, and no one could even guess their purpose. By a stroke of luck, one of our aircraft dropped a stray bomb near them, and the whole lot went up as a result of sympathetic detonation. They happened to be mines.

Although the scope of this book does not include Operation Torch, the invasion of North Africa, Douglas Kendall has given me such an interesting story connected with the planning, that I have included it:

It started with the visit of Commander Thompson, a member of Winston Churchill's staff, to Medmenham in October 1942, during the preparations for Operation Torch. Information had been received from Spain that a certain Major Garcia of the Spanish army had been instructed to bulldoze a road down to the shore a few miles west of Gibraltar preparatory to installing bolometers.

This was a device used for the measurement of all types of electro-magnetic radiation, and was invented by Samuel P.

Officers of the Army Section.
back, Toby Hick, D.
Phillips, in front Douglas Bow,
.H. Savory.

Photograph taken a week
after the St Nazaire Combined
Operations raid of 28th
March 1942. HMS
Campbeltown was used to
break down the lockgate. A =
lockgate destroyed. B = small
dam newly constructed. C =
the eastern lock. D =
damaged pump house.

Langley, American astronomer, in 1880. Originally it was intended to measure the total radiation emitted by stars, but it can also act as a highly sensitive directional detector of infra-red radiation.

Commander Thompson suspected that a bolometer was some form of measuring device capable of identifying ships passing into or away from the Mediterranean, and he pointed out that some hundreds of British and Allied ships would be moving into position before the North African landings. It would obviously have been disastrous should this vital piece of intelligence be divulged to the enemy.

Wing Commander Kendall was able to find one sortie covering the area, but there was no sign of any road, so he immediately ordered transport to Benson to obtain permission of the Senior Air Staff Officer (SASO) at 106 Group, to send a Mosquito to Gibraltar. The SASO happened to be Group Captain Peter Riddell, the creator of the Phase System of photographic interpretation who was previously in charge of the interpretation section at Bomber Command in its early days, and then posted to Wembley. The aircrew of the Mosquito took their orders for an immediate take-off, and returned thirty-six hours later with a new set of photographs showing in fact that a new road had been constructed according to the Spanish intelligence source.

In the meantime Wing Commander Kendall had deduced that the bolometers were intended to identify ships moving through the Straits of Gibraltar by means of the heat emitted from the funnels. He argued that two bolometers would be necessary, and they would have to be about 400 yards apart to be able to confirm in which direction the ships might be travelling. Douglas also argued that a bolometer would have to be sited about thirty feet above the sea-shore as it was a line-of-sight device, and would have to be above the interference caused by the earth's curvature. Equally, if the bolometer were too high, it might miss ships moving close to the shore.

To his great satisfaction, the new photographs showed two small concrete buildings parallel to each other, about thirty feet above the shore line and 400 yards apart. He plotted the two buildings on a map, and drew a line at right angles to each building in order to discover at what points they made contact on the opposite side of the Straits. Sure enough, two more buildings were identified exactly where they should have been.

Commander Thompson was presented with the report and the

D-Day + 11. Beached landing craft, boats and ships of all sizes and sections of Mulberry Harbour at the bottom of the photograph.

photographs which were shown to the Prime Minister who, in his turn, passed them to Sir Samuel Hoare, the British Ambassador to Spain. There they were placed in front of Generalissimo Franco who was outraged, saying that both road and installations had been constructed without his permission and that he would give orders to have them blown up forthwith – which they were.

I was detached from Medmenham to Norfolk House in the summer of 1942 with the vaguest possible brief, except that it was of a highly secret nature, and I presumed and hoped that it was to be a continuation of my previous work in the Airfield Section. As it transpired, I had been attached to 21st Army Group which meant nothing as I had been told nothing.

On my very first day in London I walked into Norfolk House in a state of considerable anxiety and excitement, and felt enormously relieved to see a familiar army face from CIU and was asked what I was doing there. By that time I had been able to pick up snippets of gossip, and was aware that my duties lay in the direction of planning for the invasion of northern France, so I was very cast down when the army face told me: 'Not our lot, I'm afraid, we're Torch' and pressed on up the stairs. I had not the remotest idea what he was talking about.

It seemed that the planning staff was not happy with the information regarding airfields that they were receiving from Air Ministry AI2(b) who were the recipients of the original interpretation reports from Medmenham, probably checked by me. In other words I was to check and revise AI2(b) information and submit it in a form palatable to the planners.

One of my first interpretation tasks at Norfolk House petrified me. Top Brass came in to ask me to count all new bomb craters that had appeared, probably after a softening-up attack before the Dieppe raid. No matter how many times I explained that I had never counted bomb craters in my life, it was useless and I had to do it. No comment was made regarding my report, so I never knew if it had been considered satisfactory.

From Norfolk House I joined 21st Army Group at St Paul's School Hammersmith which acted as GHQ Home Forces, and where I found myself in a most peculiar position as the only officer in light blue uniform among all the brown ones; I was billeted with ATS officers who had nothing to do with us, and I worked in a little house in Ilchester Place with a small group of army officers.

As we were walking towards the mess one day, a newcomer asked me casually 'When were you bigoted?' It was the most extraordinary question anyone had asked me, and I could not imagine what had given grounds to it. One was trained to be equivocal at moments like those, so I imagine I must have given some satisfactory answer or made a joke of it. My friends told me later that Bigot was the code name for a special security classification for which the planning staff had to be cleared, and I had never heard of it.

Twenty-First Army group needed information about airfields and landing areas for the moment when the troops were to go in. I was asked to submit preliminary reports regarding the selection and suitability of certain specific areas for landing gliders and dropping parachute troops. The reports would then be passed to the geologists for their opinion of the terrain, and receive the final assessment from other experts.

The day came when one of our number made his appearance wearing a new emblem on his sleeve – that of SHAEF. At that point I left the 'brown jobs' as the RAF insisted on calling the army, and was then posted to RAF Stanmore, still with the planners, and worked from a hut in the grounds. The work was basically the same, but this time I was to concentrate on an acceptable method of producing airfield information easily digested by Station Intelligence Officers in the field. In fact the plan was to issue them with entry books enabling them to keep an up-to-the-moment check on the conditions of landing areas as the Germans had begun obstructing these temporarily by moveable objects, and permanently by ploughing. It was also essential to know if airfields were operational and not under construction or unserviceable owing to bomb craters and damp conditions. The intelligence would have been passed on to the SIOs in a simple numerical code form.

The format I had evolved was accepted but never put to the task as there was a change in the establishment, and I was posted to AI3(c)1, the targets department at Air Ministry. It was sad for me, but it was not altogether my own fault, as in company with others, I found it difficult to accept the methods used by US intelligence officers newly arrived from the United States. The entry books had been printed in their hundreds but were never used.

As the time drew nearer to D-Day, planning shifted towards the tactical, and much of PI was undertaken by the Tactical Air Forces of the RAF and the USAAF. APIS at Medmenham were not short of work, however, as many strategic matters remained, such as the movement of enemy troops to what the Germans considered the possible battle area in northern France, and the production of their annotated maps and traces showing changes in defences. An army team had already been set up at Medmenham to assist in the vital task of locating the V-1 flying bomb launching sites in France.

Army interpreters were faced with a very large number of objects to be identified from photographs; the most important were the positions of the defence weapons of our adversaries and the type. The very fact that they were there, indicated that something of importance was to be defended, and the strength of that defence would give some idea of its importance. Anti-aircraft guns (AA) or flak guns represented the normal defence measures and by the study of comparative sorties, it was not difficult to determine the type of gun, whether heavy or light flak, from the layout of a site under construction, and when it was likely to be completed. Not unnaturally the sites followed a similar pattern.

All flak gun positions would include certain features such as huts for personnel, stacks of ammunition in the immediate vicinity of the guns, radar equipment (such as a parabaloid Würzburg), prediction controlled command posts to the side of the site, and an auxiliary command post in the centre. Disturbance of earth from the burying of underground cables connecting the command posts to the guns was the give-away. There might also be a small ammunition dump set up some distance from the gun positions. Track activity made a site very obvious.

The heavy flak guns (7.5-15.0 cms) would generally be positioned in squares of fours, or in sixes, with two light guns for their protection. The gun emplacements themselves were immediately identifiable being either square or octagonal and sometimes, when the photographs were sufficiently large scale the actual guns could be seen. The problem of camouflaging such a target was a very difficult one, as even if netting was thrown over a gun position when not in action, as soon as an alarm was given of approaching enemy aircraft, it would be dragged away offering a clear view to the camera of what was going on.

Light flak guns (2.0-5.0 cms.) were generally sited in threes without command posts and when singly would be found almost anywhere; on top of towers when among trees, or the roofs of buildings; easy to identify as the positions were square.

Searchlight sites, also in the category of anti-aircraft defence, might consist of four emplacements, each consisting of a projector and sound locator, and a light machine gun. The generator might be invisible to the interpreter, but the tell-tale underground cable leading to a building some hundred yards away from the projector to minimize interference, was a clear indication of its locality; furthermore it was always to be found at a point on the far side of the site opposite to the usual approach of enemy aircraft.

Anyone living either in cities or near particular targets in Britain during the war, will remember the balloon barrages and the comfort of their passive protection. I thought they were beautiful, those fat silver sausages up there in the skies, safely tethered to earth by their singing wires, and their underparts turning rose-coloured in the evening sun. I remember lying on the grass opposite South Kensington station near a block of flats, some having been taken over by the Auxiliary Fire Service for billets in the early days of the war, watching the balloons and listening to exciting stories of the Spanish Civil War from one of our number who had actually taken a shooting part in it, and who used to offer us good advice of what to do if machine-gunned.

Our adversaries also recognised the importance of balloons in defence, and they could be identified on aerial photographs when flown from sites near important targets. On the ground or actually flying they were unmistakable. I had almost forgotten what they looked like until recently when I was staring at a stereo pair of prints of the Sorpe Dam through my ancient stereo, and felt as if I had been hit in the face by some of those tethered white shapes.

Wire was extremely important to the interpreter as it indicated that something of a military nature was being guarded, and it was easy to identify. Disturbed soil where the supporting posts had been bashed into the ground, showed up as a series of little white dots, and working parties would leave evidence of their tracks. Even when the marks became covered by time, the results of cattle munching made the wire obvious. They would eat as far as the wire where they would have to stop, allowing the grass or nettles or whatever a chance to grow up through the wire giving a perfect outline of the area enclosed.

The interpretation of mines on aerial photographs was almost as good as the use of mine detectors, perhaps better, because as mines had to be set in the ground, the position of the ensuing white dots formed the recognisable patterns of mine laying. In one set of instructions, a rider was added to the effect that the Germans sometimes used notice boards that would not be noticed on photographs!

One of my ex-colleagues told me of a report by some inexperienced interpreter in which he had identified an ammunition dump with the usual description of dispersed units, only to discover later that it was a graveyard. The headstones had mistakenly been identified as the storage units.

The connection of the interpretation of flak sites from day photographs with those taken at night was of the utmost importance. Heavy guns would give sufficient light from firing to show ground detail, making it possible for them to be plotted on maps, and could even lead to the location of a new position previously unrecorded on day cover; also the rate of fire could be calculated from the number of salvos appearing in the form of separate pinpoints of light exposed on the negative. Light tracks from tracer flak and searchlights would also assist in plotting their own sources.

The appearance of barracks and camps, in particular prisoner-of-war camps had to be learnt, and the recognition of tanks and motor transport from their tracks or shadows. Columns of troops moving along roads were able to be detected, and, what seemed curious to me, an army PI was supposed to know what a column of horses or horse transport looked like from above. A horse in plan, they were told, had the shape of a very elongated pear.

In my ignorance I thought that military horses had disappeared from view in World War Two, and the idea that the German Command would need them in a Blitzkrieg situation seemed somehow ludicrous. However I am told that this is quite true. To save petrol, horses were used extensively behind the lines, but obviously not when success depended on the speed of an advance. My informant added that he remembered having to learn how to identify horses from above.

APIS had absolute confirmation of the excellence of their interpretation when a desperate directive from a German regimental commander was picked up near Ortona, north of the river Sangro in Italy in 1943.

These were his orders:

Coastal Defences north of Boulogne. A. Three-gun light AA. B. Minefield. C. Anti-tank ditch. D. Six-gun dual purpose AA/CD Battery. E. Command post instruments for battery (D). F. Wire obstacle.

Balloon barrage defence of the Sorpe Dam.

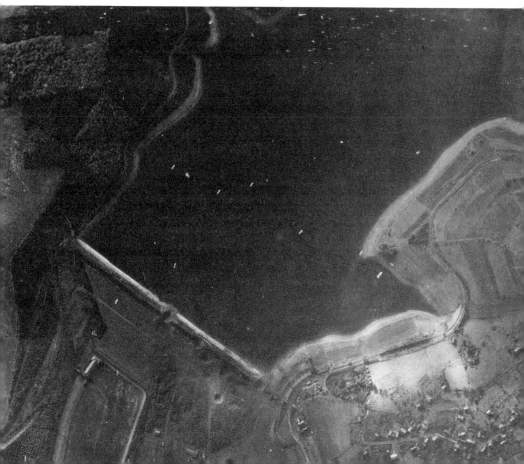

The enemy are taking photographs every day so that they know as much about our positions as any one of us. To reduce this leakage of information, you must avoid making footpaths, and you must carefully camouflage your positions. In particular you must avoid exposing your bare backsides during the daytime, as they would be clearly visible in the photographs and might pinpoint our positions.

# CHAPTER NINE

# Clipping the Wings of the Luftwaffe

Constance Babington Smith MBE was one of the few photographic interpreters able to combine a technical knowledge acquired in civilian life with the same subject in the RAF. Babs, as she used to sign herself when a journalist on the staff of *The Aeroplane* before the war, was in the happy position of being able to attend air shows and meetings in Europe, thereby having a head start over most of us who, after passing the interpretation course, had to pick up the rest of our education as we went along.

In the early days at Wembley, the identification of aircraft was undertaken by the airfield section. The squadron leader in charge was not interested in operational aircraft, and when he was posted back to Air Ministry to take over the airfield department of AI2(b) the subject was still being dealt with in a most haphazard fashion by the time CIU moved to Medmenham.

The Chiefs of Staff, finally realising the importance of obtaining intelligence regarding the strength of the opposing forces as well as the battle order, decided that Medmenham should be given the opportunity of procuring it. A separate section was formed and Babs was the obvious person to be put in charge.

Such an appointment for a woman to hold in those days was unique. The few WAAF officers who were put in charge of existing sections very quickly discovered that an RAF officer of equal rank would join them as nominal head, possibly without any technical knowledge whatsoever. However, Babs had sufficient strength of character, an extraordinary singleness of purpose together with total dedication to the task, mixed in with a modicum of determination necessary to be able to assume sole command of the new section with the rank of flight officer, which she never relinquished until after VE Day when she was posted to the Pentagon, Washington DC until the end of hostilities.

With the support of senior officers, the aircraft section was soon to be recognised as being of first class efficiency and reliability, and in addition a satisfactory relationship was built up with Air Ministry Departments and the US Enemy Objectives Unit (EOU) which dealt with the target vulnerability of the German aircraft industry. Friends at court are always useful, but never more so than in times of war when important and urgent business can be discussed informally by sensible people and opinions shared.

The first stage in aircraft identification was to count everything visible on an airfield that might fly, and then group them according to wingspan, afterwards endeavouring to identify the types present with the assistance of silhouettes specially drawn for the purpose. The silhouettes were fine as they went, but as they only showed the aircraft in plan, and as we were staring at their photographic image three-dimensionally showing all manner of curved surfaces, shadows, variations of light and funny angles, they by no means told the full story. It was found that the study of shadows was essential in the recognition of the various components of an aeroplane, and in the assessment of measurement.

On one of my many visits to the aircraft section armed with photographs of numbers of tiresome aeroplanes which it was not my business to identify even had I been able to, I remember Babs showing me an extremely clever measuring gadget of very high magnification which she used for detailed examination of her charges, and which, in those days was in addition to the standard stereos in general use.

Anything relative to wings was of great importance; among them for example, the position vis-à-vis the fuselage, the wing plan, the shape of the leading or trailing edge, the dihedral angle, and the wing span-length ratio. The number of engines was not as easy to enumerate as might be imagined, as the outline of engine nacelles of twin or multi-engined aircraft showed a tendency to fade out on small-scale photographs. Nose-shape was of great value among the recognition points, as were gun turrets to a lesser degree.

Shadows had to be treated with suspicion on occasions as they had the habit of giving an object an illusionary effect as a result of unfamiliar angles and lighting. It was often found more profitable to forget the standard rule of examining photographs with the shadows falling towards one, and turn them round to obtain a 'profile' shadow the right way up for normal viewing.

Aircraft interpreters could be bedevilled by 'light spread', this being caused by reflections from polished surfaces making objects appear larger than they should be, the outlines becoming diffused and giving a flat 'cotton-wool' look. Uncamouflaged or light-toned aircraft might be just as misleading.

Flight Officer Ursula Kay identifying the twin-jet fighter Me 262 at Lichfeld airfield.

'Seeing through camouflage'. Strips of light and dark material draped over parked aircraft.

All stereoscopic viewing of an object in motion on photographs, gives it an odd appearance owing to its blurred outline seen against a 'sharp' background, so it could be determined if an aircraft were taxying or perhaps in the process of taking off when it would be seen to 'float'.

Babs had gathered together a comprehensive selection of excellent photographs illustrating all the salient points of aircraft identification to assist the PIs; also the effects of disruptive camouflage paint, and the habit of draping strips of light and dark material over an aircraft. One set of three consecutive photographs showed a Ju88 coming in to land thus illustrating, by the distance of the aircraft from its shadow on each photograph, its height in flight.

The team at Medmenham kept themselves well up to date with the latest aeronautical developments, and in 1941 were successful in spotting a prototype FW190, technically advanced and potentially very dangerous to our side. The He280, claimed to have been the first jet aircraft in the world, was identified at Rechlin, the equivalent of the British Aeroplane and Armament Establishment at Boscombe Down. The second generation, the He280V, was seen on photographs at Rostock/Marienhe. The section was also able to confirm the truth of reports that this aircraft had been discarded in favour of the Me262, a twin-engine jet fighter carrying superior armament, and capable of a longer range. Four sad-looking He280s were revealed on a sortie covering Schwechat, the Heinkel factory near Vienna, where they had been dumped in a corner of the airfield having had their jet units removed.

The evidence of the existence of jet-propelled aircraft could be seen on the ground in the form of pairs of fan-shaped scorch marks or long dark streaks. Even if the jets themselves were absent, the proof remained, but it must have been a headache to differentiate between jets and props on such small aircraft, photographically speaking. One helpful feature was that the two small engine pods were far too close to each other to be those of propellered aeroplanes.

The only two fighter aircraft in later days which were considered successful were the Me262, already mentioned, and the Me163 (Komet) powered by a single liquid-fuel rocket showing an exhaust trail (hence its name) which was actually photographed during take-off at Zwischenahn with the trail visible. It was of a very modernistic flying-wing design, first seen at Peenemünde on 23rd June 1943. These two powerful aeroplanes caused a great deal of consternation at COS levels as the Me262 was more than 50 mph faster than the Spitfire, and the Me163 could leave the ground faster than any other aircraft in the world at that time.

An extraordinary sort of Chinese puzzle presented itself to the PIs in the sortie covering Rostock-Marienhe. At first sight it looked like a prang between two twin-engined He111s with pieces of aeroplane scattered around, but what they actually saw was the first appearance on photographs of the He111z (*Zwilling*, meaning twin). This was an amazing concoction of two He111H-6s joined together by a new wing centre on which was mounted a fifth Jumo engine, and was piloted from the port fuselage. It carried a crew of nine and acted as a tug for the vast Me321 (*Gigant*) troop-carrying glider; itself capable of transporting 200 troops and some 22 tonnes of cargo.

Naturally it was vital to discover where aircraft of the Luftwaffe were being manufactured, not only from the point of view of assessment of the order of battle, but because of the influence on target bombing priorities. Flight Lieutenant Charles Simms took over the interpretation of aircraft factories, a subject which had to be studied just like any other.

There were three main categories of factories in the aircraft industry; airframe factories, aero-engine factories, and components and assembly factories; each could be recognised by the shape of the workshops and general layout. Rather unexpectedly, the untidiness of factory workers in making heaps of such things as wings and fuselages, helped the interpreters enormously in their task of deciding what was being manufactured inside the buildings. Probably under the impression that the factories were out of range of RAF reconnaissance aircraft, the Germans constructed airfields close to the complex so that finished aircraft could be parked neatly in the open, much to the gratification of Medmenham.

Only experience could give the interpreters an idea of what was contained in the various factory buildings – for example the position of machine shops vis-à-vis the general layout, external dust extractors over fettling shops, and one of the most obvious and important of the clues were the aero-engine test beds. Buildings containing hangar test-beds when the engine would be mounted on a stand with a calibrated airscrew, were constructed in blocks, and each test-bed possessed two large square ducts for sound dispersal which were visible externally. Power beds, on the other hand, were contained in buildings grouped in sixes, and their number was more difficult to calculate. Nevertheless, the assessment of output was approximately correct. A detailed report of twenty-seven German aero-engine factories was issued on 12th January 1943 giving as much information as possible regarding the number of test-beds and the activity seen.[1]

To illustrate the importance of obtaining up to date photographic intelligence, agents' reports had been passed to MEW to the effect that the large Junkers Factory at Schonebeck was producing aero-engines; it was immediately classified as such without consulting Medmenham, and was given bombing priority. Fortunately the aircraft section had issued a report just in time stating that there was no evidence of test-beds, so an unnecessary raid did not take place.

On another occasion when the aircraft section was given no indication of a bombing priority, the result was not so happy. Although the Focke-Wulf aircraft factory at Bremen had been covered fairly frequently and reports issued, the news that the FW190 fighter, already judged to be a potentially dangerous aeroplane, was newly off the production line, never reached Medmenham, nor the intention to bomb. The raid took place on 17th April 1943 ending tragically with the loss of sixteen American bombers, although the target was successfully bombed.

The extent of the shock suffered by Chiefs of Staff can be imagined when it was realised that according to CIU reports over a three month period after the raid, there were few signs of damage being repaired. The inference was only too obvious – the factory could not have been active. Earlier sorties were combed over, and it was confirmed that production had probably ceased a short time before the raid.

Because of the importance of this new type of fighter aircraft, the factory had to be located, and whatever the cost, destroyed. The latest agents' reports were studied, and this time in conjunction with CIU, it was decided that without doubt Marienburg in East Germany was the most likely assembly point and possibly the only one. Once the interpreters had been properly briefed, they discovered that fighter production was active at the factory in 1942. A new sortie was flown, and the plant was found to have been enormously developed with an extra large hangar, a new runway, and no camouflage whatsoever. Mistakenly the Germans must have considered that the distance from Allied operational bases precluded attack.

[1] Report LS28 App I.

3          2          1

A Ju88 landing, its height being determined by the distance of the aircraft from its shadow.

Aero-Engine factory at Brunswick-Querum. 1. Test house with eight beds. 2. Two hangar beds u/c. 3. Assembly shops. 4. Hangar test beds. 5-9 are mainly machine shops.

On 9th October 1943 the Marienburg factory became the target of a very heavy raid, and post-strike photographs showed that five of the main buildings had been destroyed, leaving the place littered with the remains of FW190s.

The general situation regarding bombing priorities did not look too good from the American point of view, so in 1943, Major Kindelburg from the OSS in Washington, arrived in London with the mission to bring aircraft analysis to the notice of EOU (Enemy Objective Unit). In particular it was thought that the guidance offered to CIU was inadequate. This was very good news indeed, and almost immediately an extremely productive and satisfactory relationship was developed between the Aircraft Section and the Major. This was to be backed by another American officer, Major W.W. Rostow, already established at EOU, subsequently attached to AI2(a), and to become a member of the newly formed 'Jockey' committee.

With such powerful allies, the Medmenham Aircraft section was able to discover that certain main centres of aircraft development such as Arado, Junkers and Henschel had never been photographed, with the result that more than 50 factory airfields where prototypes were likely to appear were added to the reconnaissance programme. Intelligence began to pile up rapidly, but for various reasons such as lack of suitable long-range fighter escort for 8th and 15th USAAF daylight bombers flying deep into Germany, or bad weather conditions, the expected bombing attacks did not occur until February 1944. It was a week of fearful destruction and damage to the German aircraft industry, resulting in the subsequent dispersal of the factories, many underground so that the production of the new and successful jet aircraft could be continued.

\*

*INTERPRETATION REPORT NO. U.55*

A/c Factory Partly Underground at

# KAHLA/GROSSEUTERSDORF.

Under this heading, one of the most exciting and impressive reports I have seen was issued by the special sub-section dealing with underground factories under Captain McBride. That something as complex as the workings of a factory deep underground could be revealed by the interpretation of aerial photographs with the co-operation of the geologists at CIU, may seem impossible to the uninitiated, but the substance of the report, patiently and brilliantly researched, proves otherwise.

The project itself was the construction of an aircraft factory as remote as possible from Allied bomber bases, to be built almost entirely underground, and capable of producing wholly assembled aircraft. The location near Kahla was approximately sixty or seventy miles from the Czeschoslavakia frontier, in mountainous country thickly covered by pine forests.

The first signs of constructional activity were noticed on 26th December 1944, and by the 19th March 1945 activity on an enormous scale was continuing. If you can imagine a view from ground level, you would have seen a long, high ridge known as Walpers Berg, thrusting up from an irregular oval base with a flattened top. What immediately caught the eyes of the interpreters was that the flat top had been denuded of trees, and that a runway of over a thousand yards had been built on it. The fact that the runway was there at all could only indicate one thing – some sort of aircraft factory must be underneath it all.

The excitement at Medmenham must have been intense when the Aircraft Section was brought in to identify three aeroplanes, one waiting at the southern foot of the hill near the bottom of some sort of elevator, while the other two were parked on top near the runway. They turned out to be the important twin-jet Me262 fighters, viewed by Chiefs of Staff with concern because of their superior performance over the Spitfire. The report describes the runway as being free of obstructions due to its height, and the surface was paved and camouflaged by paint. The foundations were of the existing gravels forming a cap over the ridge.

Tunnel entrances were always a certain give-away that something was happening underground. In this case, three on the north side of Walpers Berg, and ten, with two more suspects, were identified on the south side. Electric cables of medium tension were traced in from a transformer station at Jena.

Geological conditions were reported in very great detail, giving the exact divisions of sands and sandstone of which the ridge was composed, and it was deduced which bed was the most suitable for tunnelling – also that the ridge could be opened from both sides and the entrances connected.

Five surface factory buildings were identified partly sunk into the south side of the hill with concrete roofs as a protection against bomb blast, and which had been sited on the extension of a terrace carved out of the hill, and fronting the tunnel entrances on the south side. These buildings seemed to be the most likely places for the assembly of the aircraft. The function of various other buildings could not be inferred except for the very large hutted camps of 143 barracks and possibly about 60 tents. Altogether they could accommodate 8,200 workers or twice that number according to British Army standards for the number of bunks permitted in a

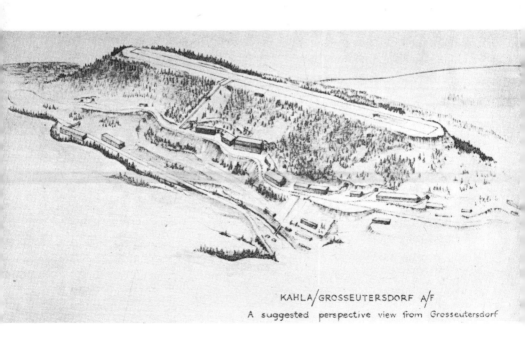

KAHLA/GROSSEUTERSDORF A/F
A suggested perspective view from Grosseutersdorf

The secrets of an underground aircraft factory at Kahla revealed from the air. Also a reconstructed ground view sketch of the site. 1. Runway, 1.135 yards. 2. Camouflage. 3. Escalator. 4. Aircraft Me262. 5. Aircraft assembly buildings. 6. Hutted camp.

specific area, and whether the bunks were single or double decked.

Narrow gauge railways had been constructed for local work, but slow progress was being made in laying a branch line from the main railway.

Water had to be made available, but rightly the PIs hesitated to make any definite statements as they could only identify ditches possibly for water pipes and a few artificial ponds, and were too well indoctrinated even to hazard a guess at the function of a 'structure resembly infiltration or sedimentation beds located near the camps'. Surely it would not have broken any rules to mention possible sewage treatment?

I must admit, excellent although this report undoubtedly is, it might perhaps have been advisable to have curbed one interpreter's use of the word 'object', and 'possible'. These following sentences go a little too far; 'Above and across three tunnel entrances can be seen an elongated object located a few feet out from the entrances. These objects resemble a bar or gantry for receiving an electric cable seen at the entrance to certain mines. 'The width of the tunnel entrances varies from approximately 8 to 12 feet, and the tunnels are entered through neatly excavated cuts on a level with the terrace or platform in front. A white object (possibly steam or smoke from a power shovel) is seen in motion in the cut leading to entrance B and a number of small black objects (possibly workers) are seen in cuts leading to two other tunnels (J and K).' These examples go to show the restraints under which the PIs had to work. White and black moving objects indeed!

This remarkable project was begun, *grâce à Dieu*, too late in the war to have been any real problem to the Allies.

## German Operational Airfields

The airfield section, of which I was in charge before being posted away in 1942, was often mistakenly identified with Constance Babington Smith's aircraft section. The only tie we had with them was in the identification of the aircraft seen on the landing areas, which they undertook. Aircraft factory airfields were also Babs' prerogative. During my time in the section, we were completely cut off from any outside information regarding the wider implications of the development of German airfields, owing to the policy of the Air Ministry Department AI2(b), the sole recipient of our reports, which was to withhold information from other sources, and that on no account were we to impart information to casual visitors to the unit. This meant working in the dark, as any friendly telephonic approach for advice to AI2(b) was frowned on. Without encouragement it was understandably difficult for our team to work with any great enthusiasm, so by a degree of badgering and even paying a visit to AI2(b) in London, I managed to create a line of communication, at least temporarily.

Our subject was as vital as any other at Medmenham, as we discovered, because we supplied information to the Air Staff, which could be used for the assessment of the order of battle of the Luftwaffe; the team being able to determine from the lay-out of an airfield under construction, the type of areoplane likely to operate from it.

Three photographs of my favourite airfield Kerlin/Bastard illustrate quite the best example of German airfield construction, and because of the excitement of watching the development of what became a very important operational base, stage by stage, and because of its name, I have never forgotten it.

The first signs that some constructional activity was going on appeared in August 1940, although we only realised this when searching for a comparative sortie. White marks had appeared instead of hedges in that closely cultivated countryside in Brittany, not far from Lorient, which meant that unfortunate French or foreign workers had to grub up the hedges. It was not until the results of a second sortie in June 1941 arrived in our section, that we realised that something very large was developing. The poor little village was completely enclosed within a perimeter track, and in the final picture in April 1943 it was totally submerged.

It was to be established later that this airfield was to serve as a base of the greatest importance for reconnaissance aircraft watching the shipping lanes, in fact the equivalent of Coastal Command, and was a back-up for the airfield at Bordeaux/Merignac.

German airfields could be divided into three main categories of fighter, bomber, and transport aircraft, and in the early pre-runway days of 1940, the size and shape of the landing areas had to be carefully calculated, as well as the size and shape of the aircraft shelters, as these factors gave a clear indication of the capability of an airfield. During the blitz on London in 1940-1941, airfields took on a different aspect with the advent of concrete runways, necessary for the operation of heavy bombers.

The first stage in planning was for a runway to be placed along

Stages in the construction of an important reconnaissance air base at Kerlin-Bastard in Brittany: 1. White lines indicate preliminary hedge clearance. 2. Early stages of runways and perimeter track construction. Notice village. 3. Second runway constructed crossing the first. Camouflage of both runways begun. Perimeter track completed with spurs leading to remote dispersal areas. Some aircraft shelters disguised as buildings almost completed – foundations of others visible. Village demolished.

one side of the landing area, to be well out of the way of any activity, and then a second stage was seen on the photographs when a second or third runway would be added in an 'A' formation within the perimeter. Sometimes a runway might be constructed, outside a landing area but meeting the perimeter, so as to obtain a maximum take-off length of about 2,500 yards, making it plain that the bomber aircraft operating from that particular airfield, would be carrying very heavy loads.

Aircraft shelters provided an accurate tally for the type of aircraft from the point of view of the size, and an assessment of the operational strength of the base by the count. At the beginning, the shelters were very basic, consisting of a horseshoe shape without a roof, but as ideas developed, they were said to have become quite luxurious with heating and water laid on. They would be arranged in units of twelve (equivalent to a squadron), and each unit would include a repair hangar with fuel and ammunition stores.

As attacks on their airfields became more frequent, the Germans dispersed the shelters sometimes miles away among houses, and built them to look like houses. This never fooled the interpreters for one minute, although they might fool pilots passing over them at great speed.

Some features which we were instructed to look for, and which could be easily identified once one knew how, were marked beacons of the 'Lorenz' blind landing system, consisting of a tiny dot with cables running to it, generally in the same position vis-à-vis the runway, and 'Visual Lorenz', which in fact was a simple lighting system for night landing.

From an interpretation point of view, the Visual Lorenz system was very interesting, as the whole enormous extent of the layout could be seen with great clarity on photographs taken in the daytime. The same old story of disturbed earth showing up white was the reason. Hundreds of poles to carry light cables were dropped into the ground at certain intervals and following a certain pattern; the base of each pole appearing white on the print. What we could see was a series of white dots approaching and in line with a runway, from a point about 6,000 yards from it; this line formed by dots, would be crossed by other dots forming short bars at varying intervals, and which could be lit independently and used as artificial horizons.

When darkness fell, the whole effect was very pretty, we were told, rather like a Christmas tree, and an absolutely marvellous guide for RAF intruder aircraft swanning around ready to beat up homing bombers. For the benefit of the navigators, all these little dots had to be plotted and traces made of them.

Flak batteries would have to be reported with the assistance of our army colleagues, as well as the condition of the camouflage of runways and aircraft shelters; road and rail facilities, fuel points, ammunition dumps, gun testing ranges, compass-swinging bases and service areas. One of the most important points of all was the condition of landing areas and runways.

During the construction stages of an airfield, the position of drainage pipes was important, and even if the airfield had been already established and operational, they were extremely easy to identify because of the herringbone pattern employed; dark patches always indicated damp ground. When, in 1945, hundreds of airfields suffered very severe bombing and the draining systems were destroyed, craters then filled with water and the airfield would become completely unserviceable.

By 1942, when the Luftwaffe were being withdrawn from Russia, it was found that there was a majority of airfields over aircraft, with the result that many had to be permanently abandoned and were ordered to be obstructed by ploughing and digging ditches; others

Basic aircraft shelters in the early years.

were obstructed temporarily by placing movable objects all over them, such as hurdles, cheveaux de frises, and tripods. The target department of Air Ministry AI3(c)1 for whom I was still working shortly after VE-day, arranged a trip in a Lancaster for some of us so that we could see for ourselves the results of the bombing in the Ruhr area. Very uncomfortable it was too, lying in the nose of the aircraft and staring down through rather dirty perspex at the horrors of destruction all round Cologne cathedral, and being astonished to see it all in colour after about four and a half years of looking at monochrome photographs. My friends were quite unable to understand why I should become so enthusiastic at the sight of some hurdles, cheveaux de frises, and tripods on one of my airfields, but I was.

# CHAPTER TEN

# Bombs Away and the Aftermath

The team of interpreters dealing with the assessment of bomb damage were still at HQ Bomber Command by the time CIU was established at Medmenham in April 1941, owing to the disagreement between Air Ministry and Bomber Command as to their ownership. It was resolved finally in September 1941, when the ten or twelve members of the team were set up in their own third phase section in the new unit.

The work of the section was of the greatest importance because the results of bomb damage influenced not only the strategic target bombing priorities, but the assessment of German industrial output, as well as the assistance to the navigational accuracy of bomber aircraft. Advice regarding damage would be requested by most of the other sections at CIU at one time or another.

Apart from the actual damage to buildings and installations, there was an impressive list of coincidental subjects for assessment and study, such as the time taken for factories to become productive after an attack, the methods of repair and reconstruction, the exact plotting of bomb craters, damage from other causes such as sabotage, the confirmation or not of ground reports, and the investigation into the capability of different types or weight of bombs.

For accurate assessment of bomb damage, large-scale photographs were essential, and if post-strike cover could be obtained within a few hours so much the better; blocked roads and uncleared debris or railway hold-ups would all indicate how much disorganization had been caused. The interpreter also needed all previous cover of a particular target with the damage reports for comparison.

The effect of fire was considered to be more serious than anything else, so the photographs had to be very carefully studied. Fresh fire damage, for example would give a whitened look to masonry, roofs would have collapsed, and when this happened the area looked like a honeycomb of lidless boxes. A curious aspect was

Chemnitz devastated by fire.

Raid on the Renault Factory at Billancourt near Paris, (*Left*) before and (*below*) after photographs.

that a large bomb say of 4,000 lbs, would tend to blow out any fires on impact. It was possible to identify furniture and other things which would have been carried out of burning houses, and piled up in heaps in streets or gardens, while fire hoses would have left pools of water in the vicinity. Quite often the full extent of the damage could not be assessed until two or three weeks after a raid, when unsafe buildings had been demolished and the debris cleared away.

As a retaliation for the broadcasts by the British traitor 'Lord Haw-Haw' from Germany, unexpected use of bomb damage experts was made by the British Government in counter-broadcasting damage to German cities in minute detail. Destruction of such familiar features as hotels and even corner shops reported by Medmenham came as a great shock to the German people.

The story of the raid by American Fortresses on the Renault Factory at Billancourt near Paris on 4th March 1942 is of particular interest, as new bombing methods were applied, and the detailed investigations by the bomb damage section into the layout and structure of the famous factory were remarkable. The raid marked the beginning of saturation bombing by USAAF Fortresses, and from the navigational and bomb aiming point of view it was ideal; the enormous plant almost totally covering the long narrow island right in the centre of the River Seine at Boulogne-Billancourt, a suburb to the south-west of Paris, so that it was a question of just following the river.

By a great stroke of luck, the Ministry of Economic Warfare managed to obtain from Lloyds who held the insurance policy, all the detailed plans of the Renault factory, and turned them over to the bomb damage section at Medmenham. The plans could not have been more fortuitous or comprehensive including as they did every factory building, vehicle assembly and engine shop, every forge foundry, and paintshop. Flight Lieutenant Ronald Gillanders (or 'Gill' as he was called) tells me that he was given the preliminary task of checking and recording all the information obtained from this windfall. Fortunately the section had fair notice of the forthcoming date of the raid, as the research took nearly three months to complete and the target material prepared.

Post-strike photographs of the factory revealed what appeared to be a shambles, and some assessments (not from Medmenham) claimed that 40% of the Renault machine tools had been destroyed. Be that as it may, the speed with which the Germans set about repairing the plant was quite remarkable, and must have had a depressing effect on the planners.

Owing to the increasing range of bomber aircraft, and improvements in navigation, the workload of the section at Medmenham grew in proportion from a strength of ten to thirteen RAF and WAAF officers in 1941 and 1942, to twenty-seven officers all told in 1943, including seven WAAF officers and six USAAF officers. The strength rose to a peak of fifty-one by April 1944 when 50% were Americans.

There was no friction between nationalities at Medmenham, and even official accounts remarked on the friendly co-operation between the Americans and the RAF. All the information and facilities were at the disposal of the Americans, and although the USAAF were responsible as far as their own reconnaissance was concerned, photographic interpretation remained centred at Medmenham.

There the Americans, having been trained initially by their more experienced colleagues, settled back to work in Bomb Damage and in the Target section. On the 1st May 1944 the station became the Allied Central Interpretation Unit (ACIU) and glowing appreciation can be found in the official *RAF Narrative of Photographic Reconnaissance*: 'Only one establishment existed until the end of the war, and in no sphere was Allied co-operation more long-standing and successful ... this indispensable part of the machinery of the strategic offensive was able to serve both forces with great and growing efficiency.'

Flight Lieutenant Andrew Lyall who was in charge of the section from 1943 to 1945 confirmed this: 'Our joint British/American set-up worked very well indeed.' The section, he told me, was always a close-knit and very happy group of people showing marked loyalty to their colleagues and the unit as a whole.

Shortage of photographic sensitized material became chronic in 1944, so the invitation of the USAAF Command that the Bomb Damage section should move to Eighth Airforce Headquarters at Pinetree, High Wycombe, where the material was more available, was gratefully accepted, and in the space of only a few hours, on 5th May 1944, all personnel were moved to what had been a very famous girls' school, and which was the source, incidentally, of a number of lewd jokes. I remember being told of one in particular which I have been assured is true.

When the building was taken over, various notices were left pinned up on the wall, and the Americans pounced on one in a dormitory (or private room?) which suggested: 'Ring if mistress required.' The sound of bawdy laughter must have been heard on the other side of the Atlantic.

The bomb damage team found itself under the command of an American officer instead of an RAF wing commander, a Major Geoff Platt. Andrew Lyall remarked, 'He was a delightful man whose attitude to us from the start was admirable. I can still recall his first words: "Andrew, I am very embarrassed about this. I know nothing of what you and your lot do, but I'll leave you alone and do all I can if you need anything." He and his brother were eminent architects from New York in civilian life.'

Pressure of work was acute with the increase of the bombing, and many changes in the organisation had to be met. It was also found, that it had become almost impossible to put any time aside for training newcomers, until someone dropped a clanger which brought things to a head. Far away in the United States a person added a digit to a requisition form for officers to be trained as metereologists for the USAAF, resulting rather naturally in ten times as many eager young American officers as required. 'So we got a group of the excess sent to us with no PI knowledge whatsoever,' Andrew commented, 'and somebody had to run a training school for them. John Holder agreed to do this, and did a better job than anyone else could have done ... he won the regard and the affection of the trainees, and this particular group became, like our earlier Americans, admirable interpreters well versed in our techniques. A remarkable achievement on John's part as they were all very browned off when they reached us.'

Medmenham had another useful invention up its sleeve in the form of the 'Damometer' which was an extremely ingenious aid to overworked bomb damage interpreters. Alick Heron invented it, designed and constructed it; no one seems to know how it earned its name, and its job was to assess large areas of damage in built-up areas. It was not intended to deal with detailed damage of a specific target.

The apparatus was not exactly elegant in appearance, however elegant the design, but it earned high praise in Washington where its properties were considered almost magical. Although it did not do anything that had not been done before it came on the scene, any bomb damage interpreter who had the tedious and time-consuming job of measuring up total areas of damage in a badly damaged city would agree that the Damometer saved hours of soul-destroying work.

This clever instrument was capable of determining the net acreage of a given area, i.e. that covered by buildings alone, and because it could measure the area of both damaged and un-damaged buildings, it could calculate the percentage of property seriously damaged or destroyed. A fixed stereo viewer was built into the instrument, under which the stereo prints could be moved, either vertically or horizontally, in straight lines, scanning the selected area. Distances were able to be measured in millimetres by a pointer travelling over either damaged or undamaged areas; and as the scale of the photograph was known, these could be converted into real life measurements. A more sophisticated addition later was an electrically controlled scriber automatically recording in diagrammatic form, a plan of the built-up areas of the town and the damage inflicted.

Medmenham's bomb damage section evolved a new system of presenting bomb damage to their 'clients' consisting mostly of the Americans, heavily involved in saturation bombing by day from 1943. This was the production by a lithograph process of damage plots made up from a 1:25,000 scale photographic mosaic or photographic map of, for example, an area including two towns somewhere in the industrial part of Germany. The towns were bombed on two separate dates, and the area of damage was indicated in red for the first raid, and in blue for the second; simple and very effective. These and the result of the statistical measurements of the Damometer were a great step towards obtaining intelligence quickly and efficiently.

Flight Lieutenant W.A. Seaby (Bill) was asked to take over the 'Special Jobs' when the section moved from Medmenham to Pinetree; these were the assessment of damage inflicted on a particular target by exceptionally large bombs, or experimental bombs – targets such as the U-boat shelters, with their 12 feet plus thick reinforced concrete roofing, and the Möhne and Sorpe dams, the mysterious 'Heavy Sites' in northern France connected with the V-weapons, railway viaducts in Germany, and a railway tunnel near Saumur. These heavy 'aerodynamic missiles' the brain children of Barnes Wallis were capable of deep penetration, and had delayed action fuses. Much valuable help was received from RE8 (Research and Experiments Department 8, Ministry of Home

(*right*) The 'Damometer' with
inventor, Alick Heron.
(*below*) Bielefeld railway
viaduct destroyed by Tallboy
and Grand Slam bombs, the
photograph showing the
pattern of their enormous
craters.

Security), and from other armament sources. In the early stages each Tallboy five-ton bomb dropped, was numbered, whether or not its impact had been located on the ground, so that by the time of the third raid on Brest U-boat pens on 13th August 1944, the numbers were well into the hundreds.

Air Vice-Marshal G.A. Pidcock, Vice-President of the (Air) Ordnance Board was instrumental in Bill Seaby (known as the 'crater chaser') joining two missions to France and one to Germany for the purpose of first-hand study of damage to installations inflicted by heavy calibre bombs designed by Barnes Wallis. The bombs were 'Upkeep' the Bouncing Bomb of four tons; 'Tallboy' of five tons, and 'Grand Slam' of ten tons.

Saumur Tunnel on the main line railway in the beautiful châteaux country of Touraine, was the first strike of 617 Squadron using Tallboy bombs, and the mission was anxious to check the depth of the principal crater, and the amount of spoil it might have removed. The bomb in question had landed right over the tunnel, pierced the roof and blown an enormous hole in the stonework; the sablon, which was a mixture of sand and clay, had fallen back as a great spallheap above the tunnel roof. A more comprehensive manner of blocking a tunnel would be hard to imagine, and the effort needed to repair the damage was phenomenal. It took from the 9th June to 25th July 1944 to remove thousands of cubic metres of loose spoil with all the earth moving equipment available, and to fill in other huge craters which had cut the railway lines.

While on the subject of railway targets, the mission also visited the marshalling yard of Trappes, south-west of Paris, which had been plastered by bombs during the intense fighting in this region after D-day. The extent of the damage astonished even the members of the mission; the large numbers of locomotives destroyed, carriages and trucks burnt out and disrupted railway lines. Craters were still unfilled in September 1944 although some clearance was being carried out by the French.

The mission to Germany consisting of Air-Vice Marshal Pidcock, Barnes Wallis, two group captains, one wing commander, one flight lieutenant (Bill Seaby) and LAC Hart to take the photographs to illustrate the report, left the UK in April 1945. Among the number of targets visited and the results of the damage of Tallboy, Grand Slam and Upkeep bombs assessed at first hand were the Möhne and Sorpe dams, the Dortmund-Ems Canal and the twin railway viaducts of Bielefeld crossing the River

The Möhne Dam breached. The arrow indicates the remains of the torpedo boom.

Werre and carrying the main line from Berlin to the Ruhr.

This target had been of the highest priority, and had been extensively bombed prior to 14th March 1945 when thirteen Tallboys and one Grand Slam were dropped, and to illustrate the extraordinary efficiency of the Germans in repairing damage, it was noticed from aerial photographs, that a loop line had been constructed before the big ones were dropped and three days after, a train of flat wagons could be seen crossing the exact place which had formerly been an enormous bomb crater.

There still exists one of the finest and most dramatic pictures taken of bomb damage, at least in my view. As can be seen in the illustration, it is a most vivid, awsome low-angled shot of the double viaduct at Bielefeld showing the arches stretching right across the print like a row of teeth with a gap of about six arches width in the centre, and festooned between this gap are delicate strands formed by two railway lines still attached to the ends of the gap. Enormous circular puddles surround this aiming point for hundreds of square yards, as these are the craters of Tallboy and Grand Slam bombs, with great numbers of minor heavies. There is a row of little houses still with their roof structure apparently intact, but with most of the tiles gone – not surprisingly. Stereo pairs of prints taken in sequence during a strike were obtained, showing for the first time the whole development of a strike in stereo.

During the mission, much of the time was taken up in identifying the craters made from the bombs which Bill Seaby had numbered in the interpretation reports, and must have been a formidable task. Barnes Wallis showed his appreciation by congratulating the ACIU team for their accurate assessment of the capability of the giant bombs which he himself had predicted, but had been over-cautious in not expecting any one bomb to land within a few yards of the aiming point.

### Night Photography Interpretation

The most important task asked of interpreters post-strike was to discover from photographs taken during the day, if aircraft of Bomber Command had been successful in reaching their targets, or had failed. This the Bomb Damage section was able to achieve; however, the same problem of navigation remained during night raids. Photographs taken during night attacks were also proof of success.

Experimentation led to the employment of photographic flash

photograph taken with
over Courtrai 31st May
0.

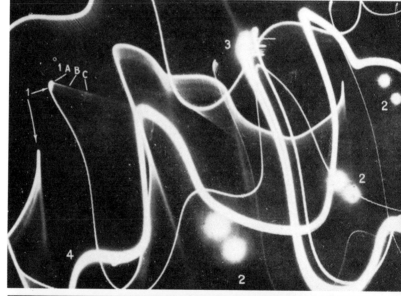

tracks over
mund. (1) Two typical
chlight tracks. (1A) The
itself (1B) and (1C)
ls on the beam due to
of mist and haze. (2)
-gun salvoes from a
y battery. (3) Tracks of
burning among houses.
rack of fire at decoy site.
mund/Ellinghausen. The
rent changes of direction
e beams are due to
ve action by the aircraft.

Officer Loyalty Howard
he 'nesting box' used for
g fire plots.

bombs synchronised to fire in space, at the moment of impact of the HE bomb on the ground, which had been dropped from the same aircraft which carried the camera. The wide area of light produced around the bomb burst would enable recognisable features such as streets and other landmarks to be identified, and the position plotted on a map.

A great deal of research into cameras, photo-flash fuses and bomb release circuits was undertaken to perfect the system, while the PI or interpretation side of the subject, which was particularly specialised, was evolved by Bernard Babington Smith, (Babs' brother), who was first stationed at No 3 PRU at Oakington in Bomber Command. The unit was closed down in 1941, the operational side being transferred to Benson, while the personnel of the photographic interpretation section under Flight Lieutenant Babington Smith moved to Medmenham, and was established by February 1942.

Bernard had discovered at Oakington that a great deal of vital information could be obtained from night photographs, other than that by the photo-flash. The reason for this was that the camera worked on the open-shutter principle of exposure, causing images of other light sources to appear on the film before and after the moment of the operation of the flash bomb. The camera worked on the open-shutter principle and because of this, the images of direct light sources such as fires on the ground or flak shining *directly* into the lens, would appear on the film both before and after the moment of operation of the flash bomb in the air, which had the job of illuminating the scene below and whose light would be *reflected back* into the lens.

A direct source of light appears as a dot on the film when a fixed camera and a fast shutter-speed is used, but in the case of a flying camera and an open shutter, the same source of light makes a streak on the negative appear rather like a piece of spaghetti on the print.

Bernard realised that a curious phenomenon existed in that each source of light could be identified by its particular light streak, and from measurements, useful observations could be made; the type and intensity of flak, for example, the size and duration of fires; the spacing and method of the operation of searchlights, the layout and duration of decoy targets, length of flare paths, visual landing aids and flashing beacons connected with airfields. Particularly useful to the Army Section was the ability to record the position of gun

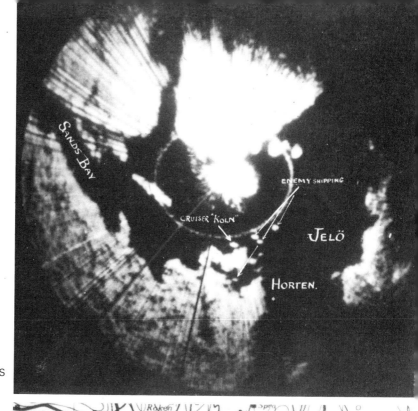

Photograph taken of an H2S screen during an operation against enemy shipping in Oslo Fjord the night of 13th/14th December 1944.

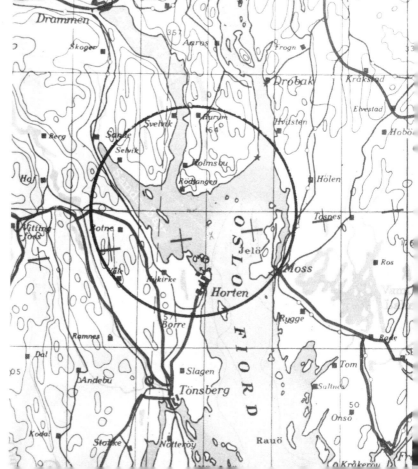

battery sites and the number of salvos fired, and once the bomb burst were plotted on maps, it made it easier for the bomb damage section to locate and assess damage on post-strike cover.

To most of the uninitiated like myself, Bernard and his team seemed to work and live in a sort of magician's cave, festooned with yards of processed and sometimes unexposed film for tracing purposes, surrounded by hundreds of containers or cans, and a light box for examining film when making fire plots, and which Loyalty Howard, then a flight officer in the section, tells me was christened the nesting box. What these people were doing or looking at made me feel supremely uneasy, probably because I was a professional photographer, and it seemed to go against all the principles of photography as I knew it, and I understood nothing of their ploys. In fact, at the time Bernard sounded rather on the defensive towards his brain child, when he wrote in a report that the great majority of night photographs would not stand comparison, photographically speaking, with those taken for reconnaissance, and that it could not be stressed too highly, that whatever faults they might have, they brought back information of the utmost value.

The use of $H_2S$ as a navigational aid, also turned out to be an aid to interpreters as it was possible to photograph the actual radar display on the screen in the aircraft during a raid, thus giving its exact position. When Bernard Babington Smith told me recently, that the interpreters were able to estimate the grouping or concentration of aircraft during a raid, and even the way the attack was developing, in conditions of ten-tenths cloud, I thought he was joking, but it was not so; the interpretation of cloud pattern was the secret. It was possible to plot the position of aircraft by the pattern of the clouds they each recorded on film.

An important refinement was added when the Pathfinder Force was created. Their job was to fly over the target and drop coloured markers or Target Indicators for the guidance of their colleagues in the following bomber aircraft, and what soon became apparent to the interpreters, was that these meant more white streaks to identify on the film. The solution to this problem was very ingenious indeed; it was the use of colour film in conjunction with black and white film, which also helped to differentiate between normal fires and incendiaries, and made it easier to detect decoy fires.

At that particular time in the war, at the beginning of 1944, colour film was very scarce, so some clever people decided that it would be possible to use only two colour frames in a length of black and white film to be exposed. This length of colour film which equalled the area of two frames was physically glued onto the emulsion side of its supporting black and white film thus shielding its sensitised support from exposure by the backing of the colour film – a brilliant innovation.

# CHAPTER ELEVEN

# The Life Blood of German Industry
## Applying the Torniquet

The Industry section was established soon after the interpretation unit arrived at Medmenham in 1941, under Flight Lieutenant Hamshaw-Thomas (later to become Wing Commander in charge of Third Phase). There was a great need for information regarding the output of the enemy war material, because after it had been assessed, it contributed towards the allocation of targets on the bombing programme.

The work was extremely specialised entailing a comprehensive knowledge of metals, electrical equipment, engineering, textiles or chemicals; while on the subject of power, interpreters were required to become authorities (if they were not already so in civilian life) on oil, coal, or electricity leading to dam construction. The team worked in close collaboration with the Bomb Damage Section who were able to assess the likelihood of a plant returning to production after a raid.

One of the tasks was to locate factories, and often this meant months of meticulous research wading through street and telephone directories, referring to ground reports and collaborating with the Wild Section for the production of plans.

An example of the mammoth quantity of study required for one subject only, was the issue of power grid maps covering the whole of France and Germany, and entirely made up from aerial photographs; the tracing of power lines being extremely useful in establishing the locality of previously unknown factories. This same task brought to light an unfortunate breakdown in communication with an outside source of intelligence, as someone neglected to inform Medmenham until the project was completed, that a map of power transmission lines in France already existed.

The arrival of US officers in the Industry Section in 1943 was welcomed, as they integrated well and worked away contentedly with their British colleagues as they did in the rest of CIU.

The team was fortunate in being able to obtain information from the American Committee of Operations Analysts which possessed facilities for communicating with some of the most influential firms in the United States, and from US agencies in close touch with MEW and other government offices. Furthermore, the committee was able to get in touch with American specialists in engineering and construction, and who in some cases had helped to build the plants to be attacked.

As the analysis of German oil production was of crucial importance (indeed some critics remarked that if it had been given top bombing priority, the war might possibly have ended a year earlier) a sub-section was formed to deal with it, and to answer to a joint Oil Targets Committee composed of representatives of Bomber Command and Intelligence Directorates, MEW, the Enemy Objectives Unit of the US, and the War Office.

One of the members of the team was Peter Kent,[1] a young geologist held in high regard not only by his superior officers at Medmenham, but from those in top ranking positions outside the unit; in fact the Combined Strategic Committee of 2nd May 1945 stated as regards enemy oil production that the main responsibility for the final photographic appreciation was borne by an officer of the RAF of junior rank, P.E. Kent, and to whose exceptional talent high tribute was paid by the oil committee.

One of the first tasks when the new section was established at Medmenham, was the location and measurements of oil storage tanks captured by the Germans in the occupied territories. To the interpreters, storage tanks were easily identified because of their basic shape, and because they would be surrounded by earthen banks or blast walls against fire and high explosives. Most would have flat roofs, but for the storage of highly volatile oils, floating roofs could be expected. The idea was that they should float on the surface, which offered the PIs a most unexpected clue as to the quantity left in the tank; a ladder would be pivoted against the side of the tank, and when it was full, it would lie horizontally on top of the roof, in clear view of the camera. As the level dropped obviously the ladder would gradually incline.

Quite early on there were signs too that enormous underground storage installations were being constructed, which, when completed, consisted of reservoirs built of concrete with a capacity of about twenty to forty tons of oil in each. They would be completely buried in groups, and the area covered over by a layer of

---

[1] Now Sir Peter Kent D.Sc., FRS.

soil and planted trees and bushes. Had it not been for the fact that the constructional activity had been watched throughout, and that ventilators sometimes showed above ground, the underground installations would have been almost impossible to discover.

It soon became apparent that the main oil sources were to be found in Germany, and cover of the Schleswig Holstein and Hanover oilfield areas combined to bring up to date the knowledge of indigenous natural hydro-carbon sources and the small refineries from which they fed.

The oilfields themselves were never targets, as they were difficult to damage effectively, and the refineries were so small, that they attracted little attention until late in the war. The most outstanding features of an oilfield were the derricks and tanks or pits for circulating liquids, the shadows simplifying the PIs job.

The main sources were in fact sixteen synthetic oil plants which were being constructed widely across Germany and the occupied territories wherever coal, lignite (brown coal) or tar were available as feed stock; as the earlier plants had been established mostly in the Ruhr which had been photographed frequently, the knowledge of the processes and plant layout was built up from an early date.

Two processes were in general use for the production of synthetic oil, the Fischer Tropsch gas synthesis process, and the Bergius process which treated coal, coal tar, creosote or heavy oil by combining the carbon content of these substances with hydrogen to produce oil and petrol.

The interpreters had a considerable advantage in the knowledge that the patents for hydrogenation of coal were internationally owned by the German IGF, British ICI, and US Standard Oil, which enabled them to turn to ICI for advice regarding the German operations and methods. Furthermore, the Germanic insistence on order, resulted in precise layout for each operational unit, making it a comparatively easy task to identify particular sections of a plant.

Each type of plant could be recognised by its characteristic features: for example the gas synthesis Fischer Tropsch by its gas holders, sulphate removal plant, and a large tall building containing contact ovens in which the synthesis took place: and the hydrogenation Bergius plants by their high concrete or brick roofless structures, open on one side, containing the synthesis vessels, gas plants of many sizes, and a large building containing hydrogen compressors. Common to both would be the cooling towers, a large power station and boiler plant, oil tanks and

Updating the records of oil production, damage to plants, dates of attacks and photographic cover.

The Industry Section.

refining equipment. The gas plants were the most vulnerable parts of any oil synthesis plant, as they were easily damaged and highly flammable; both types were frequently situated at a pit head or near a brown coal mine.

One of the most exciting discoveries by aerial photography was that of the enormous plant at Brux near the Czechoslovakia frontier in 1942. The first indications that such a project existed were advertisements for oil engineers appearing in a German technical magazine, and ground reports suggested that the output might reach 240,000 tons per annum, but there was no information regarding its location or size.

Photographic cover was laid on immediately in May 1942, and the interpreters were able to confirm that a very large synthetic oil plant was under construction. They also discovered an alarming situation which was that the plant was nearing completion; an enormous project occupying a site about one and a half miles square. Other sources confirmed that it was designed for an initial production of 750,000 tons per annum, which would make it equal to the largest plant in the world, and it was likely to come on stream in about six months.

A second sortie eleven months later revealed that the plant was operational, and that the production was at the rate of 20% of the total assessed output. An added anxiety was the realisation that the equipment installed up to 1942 was only the first stage in the construction, and that extensions were already beginning to increase the potential output, and as the successive items of the plant were brought into operation, all that the Medmenham interpreters could do was to watch this alarming progress towards the possible maximum output in early 1944.

Some interesting and unusual observations were made in the interpretation of some plants; for example at Brux, a half mile long air intake pipe to the gas plant was provided with a large enough diameter to drive a small car into it, indicating the degree of air pollution in the plant; and at Politz hydrogenation plant near Stettin, what was believed to be signs of operational activity from wisps of steam seen on the photographs, showed, on closer inspection that steam had, in fact, been put through the pipe lines all round the works to help trace leaks needing repairs.

Observations of this kind were made possible by the remarkable quality of the photographs taken by PRU by which it was possible for the interpreters to pick out even the expansion joints on pipe

Part of Brux synthetic oil refinery – then the largest in the world. May 1942.

bridges within the plants, the individual pipe connections of high pressure compressors, or a messenger on a bicycle leaving the works' gate. Admiration for the courage and skill of the pilots and aircrew was unbounded as they flew hundreds of miles over enemy territory in unarmed Spitfires or Mosquitos, and it was largely due to the risks they took that estimates of production were sufficiently accurate for practical use.

What was considered the most important objective next to oil production was that of electrical energy, resulting in the investigation into thermic and hydro-electric power installations; the interpreters having to make themselves familiar with the main features and layout of both types. By the beginning of 1943 Barnes Wallis' persistence succeeded in convincing the powers that be that his Bouncing Bomb made the bombing of the great dams of Möhne, Eder, and Sorpe practicable and they were given top bombing priority. Medmenham was required to submit details of construction, water levels, defences and Wild plans, as well as scale models.

The first photographic cover of the dams was in February 1943, and thereafter sorties produced regular cover for the preparation of the attacks on 17th May 1943.

Strategically speaking, the results of the attacks on the dams were considered disappointing. It is true that main railway lines were disrupted for some time, many bridges being destroyed, and production was affected by water shortages, but only temporarily. Some electrical plants were destroyed, coking plants in Dortmund lost 9% of their production over two months, but repairs were unbelievably swift; the dams were back into commission before the winter rains. The loss of life was fearfully high, over a thousand people being drowned or missing, and acres of pasture land flooded.

During the summer of 1944 the Industry Section found itself unknowingly and marginally concerned in the search for evidence regarding the possible employment of nuclear reaction by the Germans in the manufacture of an atomic bomb. It was common knowledge in intelligence circles that the production of heavy water, which acts as a moderator for slowing down neutrons in an uranium pile, was being undertaken at the Norsk plant at Vermork in Norway, successfully raided by a party of Norwegians and British Commandos in February 1943, and now it seemed that something else was in the offing.

Douglas Kendall, who was Wing Commander Technical Control Officer, was approached by ADI(Sc) regarding a possible base for German nuclear activities established in a large country house in or around Hechingen near Stuttgart. In fact, agents reported that Werner Heisenberg, nuclear physicist, and his colleagues were working there.

The brief was vague as the only information available to help photographic interpretation was that the Manhattan Project in the USA (where all the Allied efforts in this field were concentrated) was a very large plant requiring great quantities of electric power, and a lot of water for cooling purposes.

Special photographic sorties over the area in Germany could be laid on if necessary, and Douglas, as officer in charge of these operations, was to be the sole individual in the know. He decided to use the industry section for the investigation, and his instructions must have left the interpreters wondering. First they had to plot on a map all the power stations in Germany, and then trace all the powerlines from the generating stations to final points where they entered a possible plant. This was easier than might have been expected, as the transmitter power had to be broken up at transformer stations, and then re-distributed to other lines; by examining and measuring the transformers, it was possible to calculate the load being switched to each line. A big consumer would have its own transformer station, making it possible to assess the power entering an individual plant.

The idea was that they would plot the transmission lines in the whole of Germany, and attempt to account for the total consumption, but the big worry was that photographic cover of the whole country at a scale of 1:10,000 necessary for that type of interpretation, just did not exist.

The section then had the job of plotting all existing cover over the suitable areas, making it possible to find the gaps in coverage, and to fill up these gaps, photographic sorties were laid on with high priority.

Douglas Kendall examined all the houses in the Stuttgart area, but none looked suspicious. There were no new power lines nor new buildings which might indicate questionable activity, nor any new plants of questionable size which could be accounted for. However, towards the end of the investigation, something quite extraordinary turned up.

Fourteen new plants of identical design were located out in the country. All of them showed the beginning of pit operations; there was a grid laid out on the ground over which had been piled material from the pit; a chimney and an oil storage tank. By close scrutiny, Douglas discovered that all these mysterious plants seemed to be located on the same contour level, the logical assumption being that they were somehow connected with the material dug out of the pits. The next step was to send one of the Medmenham geologists to study the area on German geological maps, available in a London museum. He found that all the plants were in fact located on a thin band of oil shales.

A Swedish source offered the information that oil recovery from shales was being undertaken in Sweden, and the conclusion was that this must have been the sole purpose of the fourteen new plants.

Three months were spent on this mammoth task in order to be able to report to ADI(Sc) that there was no indication *from aerial photographs* available at Medmenham that the Germans were working on the production of an atomic bomb at that time although Hechingen became the main centre for atomic research in early 1945.

## *Transportation of the Goods*

As soon as the War Office became aware of the need for intelligence regarding troop and freight movements, a civilian official of the London and North Eastern Railway of Great Britain, Mr R.J. Moody, was given a commission as staff captain (TN) in the Royal Engineers. Shortly after CIU had been established at Medmenham in April 1941 Captain Moody was made officer-in-charge of the new Communications Section (or Transportation as it became known).

Ron Moody battled away on his own to begin with, endeavouring to obtain as much reference material as possible, such as continental railway guides, time-tables, diagrams and maps. The first reports contained details of facilities and locations and particulars of rolling stock, and the advent of four RAF officers to his section in June 1941 enabled him to widen the scope of interpretation to include waterways. The War Office decided to increase the establishment by three sapper officers from the RE Railway Depot at Longmoor in September 1941.

Most of the reports were issued in the form of weekly summaries giving information regarding railways and waterways, military traffic and details of loadings at vital points.

As bombing raids on railway centres intensified, bomb damage

ectrified railway at Oslo.
rows indicate gantries.

arshalling yards at Vaires
ar Paris after heavy
mbing.

Officer, surrounded by
way timetables and books
eference, reporting on
pzig railway terminus.

assessments were required; the establishment was increased, and Second Phase interpretation as early as 1942 was issuing damage reports of marshalling yards in France. Bombing priorities were largely controlled by the concentration of rolling stock and flats loaded with military equipment.

The interpreters had to have a working knowledge of the technicalities of railway transport; for example, it was vital to be able to recognise how trains were made up, or if a line was electrified (simple enough, as gantries would be seen quite clearly); and a useful clue as to which country the trains were travelling in, was the habit of the traffic in Holland and Germany to travel on the right, while in the others, it would be directed to the left.

Not surprisingly, marshalling yards and sidings were considered the most sensitive and vulnerable parts of the whole system, being the nerve centre for freight traffic, and where the greatest concentration of rolling stock would be found. Many had a total length of two miles with sixty or more separate tracks, and the capacity for handling thousands of wagons a day. The method of working marshalling yards was either manual, when trains were sorted and divided by shunting locomotives and man-power, or by mechanisation with the assistance of the 'hump'. For some weird reason, I have always remembered this hump which I must have met during my PI course. It was a raised section from which a train of trucks to be sorted would be despatched down a gentle slope towards the sorting sidings; the speed and switching being controlled electrically from a cabin near the hump. It stands to reason that a bomb dropped on or near the hump would cause maximum damage as the whole system would be thrown out of order.

The Germans were so efficient at repair work to the railways, that effective strategic bombing by the Allies was impossible; however when the invasion became imminent, the railway system assumed a tactical level being the target for both medium and heavy aircraft. At this stage, First Phase undertook not only urgent reports, but more detailed intelligence. Successful bombing had a serious effect on the production and delivery of the enemy's war material as the rolling stock diminished, and in February 1944, by the time the first heavy bombing attacks were directed against French marshalling yards, the system was stretched to the limit.

As a result of close investigation, the interpreters soon noticed that seriously damaged or destroyed railway bridges and viaducts took much longer to repair than marshalling yards, and must have been another factor towards the shift of transport from the railways to the waterways when feasible, so as to maintain the flow of vital war material to and from the Ruhr. In Germany, inland waterways had reached an advanced stage of development. The chief rivers of the Rhine, Ems, Weser, Elbe and Oder, flow more or less from south to north, and were linked by an east-west canal system giving a through connection from Holland to East Germany.

The main traffic consisted of 300 ft self-propelled barges, while barges without engines could be seen in tows behind paddle tugs. One convoy of particular interest consisting of pairs of 140 foot barges boarded together, was noticed near an aircraft factory, and on three occasions a single Ju52 was spotted on a double barge. Because of the enormous increase in freight transport, inland ports were created at Duisburg, Mannheim and Cologne among others; Veltenhof in particular was equipped with excellent docking facilities.

France and the Low Countries possessed a well developed canal and river network linking sea ports with inland areas; ship canals being capable of accommodating up to 30,000 tons; the Nieuwe Waterweg (North Sea Canal) and the Ghent-Terneugen were examples of these. In north-eastern France a characteristic feature was the 'garage' or assembly point for barges.

Our interpreters had to be well informed regarding the most vulnerable points for air attack which, in the main, consisted of aqueducts (the most difficult to repair and very easy to identify) locks, ship-lifts, and bridges carrying railways or roads over canal embankments. Different types of locks were there to be studied, such as the 'guillotine' with a gate instead of a knife; the retractable gate which could be drawn sideways into the embanked area; the old fashioned 'V' lock when the two gates meet in the middle, and which everybody travelling along the rivers and canals of the UK must have come across, and a fourth type which looks to me like the forerunner of the 'up and over' modern garage door.

I would have liked to have been a passenger on one of the barges when it was lifted sometimes 60 feet to find the new level of water in a higher canal, if it could have been possible, as it must have been very exciting. The barge would be manoeuvred into a tank within an elaborate lifting gear, the tank would be closed and the whole lot elevated. Electric power would be used for this operation, and the small power house was always visible to the interpreter.

# CHAPTER TWELVE

# Mysteries of the Air Waves
## Plotting the Sources

Britain was woefully behind the Germans, at the beginning of the war, in radar experimentation and development, and it is to be regretted that the scientists of the moment rejected the information handed to them by the unknown author of a remarkable document known as the 'Oslo Report'.

On 5th November 1939 a package was left on the windowledge of the British Consulate in Oslo. Inside was a report written in German revealing the full extent of the German military scientific research, including such subjects as radar direction finding systems, with instructions how to counteract the signals, and descriptions of the installations themselves; even mentioning an electric dish for the purpose of transmitting short electric pulses, which was later to be known as the 'bowl fire' after it had been discovered by the Radar Section at Medmenham.

Academic arguments on the accuracy of the report took place behind the scenes, but in December 1939 open interest was shown after the Battle of the River Plate in Montevideo when the pocket battleship *Graf Spee* was scuttled. Whitehall received a report that an unusual aerial array had been noticed above the optical range finder, and a British radar expert was despatched forthwith to investigate the mystery. He returned with the news that, in his view, the strange installation was a form of rotary radar probably being used for gun-laying purposes. No further investigations took place, and the report from the radar expert was safely tucked away, until 1941 when intelligence officers were given the information.

By a happy coincidence, a friend of Lemnos Hemming, the managing director of AOC at Wembley, asked if he could join the unit. Claude Wavell was a brilliant mathematician and had been engaged in an air survey of Rio de Janeiro, so his application was received with enthusiasm and he was asked to concentrate on the interpretation of W/T on photographs.

As early as September 1940 a Knickebein Navigational Beam Transmitter had been identified near Cherbourg, a discovery that caused a great deal of interest in the scientific circles at Air Ministry intelligence.

A Knickebein transmitter was a member of an odd quartet known as the 'offensive' transmitters, the other members being called Ruffian, Benito, and Windjammer. They were built after war was declared, and christened 'offensive' because they acted as navigational aids to German aircrew flying on bombing missions over Britain.

The most important of this group was the Knickebein which was made in two sizes, the giant and the small, and could be identified on photographs by what looked to be a circle crossed centrally by a bar, and which in fact was a turntable on which was fixed the aerial array. The giants were seen to have turntables of about 300 feet in diameter and an aerial of 90 feet high, while the small Knickebein had a base of about 100 feet supporting aerials of 40 feet high.

The next discovery by Squadron Leader Wavell, or 'Wavey' as he was affectionately known by all of us, was in November 1940 when a Freya Radar station[1] was identified near Audeville on the Hague Peninsula. The Freya was a member of the Defensive group so named as its function was to detect hostile aircraft. On vertical photographs, it also had a circular appearance, as it consisted of a small hut about 7 feet square, with a 'cross-bar' or aerial array fitted above it, and the whole surrounded by a circular blast wall; there might be several such units close together. The most exciting feature from the interpreters' point of view, was that the aerial was capable of rotating, and they actually saw this occur on the photographs, by the change of the width of the shadow on a stereo pair.

Among some of the papers preserved after Claude Wavell's death, are notes in which he wrote that the observation about the movement of the aerial settled a controversy then still raging in authoritative circles, as to whether radar was being used by the Germans. 'It was,' he wrote, 'the first step of unravelling the intricate network of what proved to be radar, at practically every stage of which photographic interpretation took the lead and provided clues long before they were forthcoming from other sources.'

The Freya was not alone in its direction finding activities, as there was a second widely used type of RDF equipment, known to

[1] Or RDF (radio direction finding) stations.

the Germans as the Würzburg (also in two sizes), described so accurately in the Oslo Report of 1939 and which was unknown to Squadron Leader Wavell until some time during 1941 when hints were received from Air Ministry as to its appearance and possible layout. This group was termed 'defensive'.

Although CIU had been established at Medmenham since April 1941 Claude still did not have an independent section; although his team had been considerably increased, they were still part of a sub-section of Second Phase when a sortie was flown over a place called Cap d'Antifer, NNE of Le Havre and near the village of Bruneval, in August 1941. Many months had been spent searching for a paraboloid installation called a Würzburg (and unofficially a bowl fire), and it was quite by chance that the sortie was passed to the Radar team by the Army Section who had prior pecking order because of their brief to study coastal defences. APIS investigated something that might have been a gun position, decided it was not, and that it might have something to do with radar, and for want of a better idea passed it along to Wavell's section.

Interpretation of the photographs was not easy, as they were what was known as 'high level obliques' and not verticals; taken from a long way off and very small scale. The object rejected by the Army looked like a small dot on a cliff top, and was only a few hundred yards from two Freyas which had already been plotted. Because of the general layout, and because of the track activity leading to it from the two Freyas and continuing towards a largish villa which must have been used as headquarters for the whole radar complex, Claude realised that the very small dot would have to be a paraboloid installation. A report to this effect was immediately sent to ADI(Sc) and a sortie was subsequently flown resulting in some of the most remarkable close-ups of the war. The existence of the Würzburg was confirmed.

In preparation for the famous Bruneval raid on 27th February 1942 the Army Section had to investigate every inch of the terrain to locate defences and study topographical features for parachute drops, and the Model Section produced a wonderful representation of the villa and the bowl fire, from information received from other sections at Medmenham; this can be seen in the photograph on page 65.

The Freyas, being the first apparatus of the group of radar direction finding stations to appear, were established at nearly all the Early Warning Aircraft Reporting stations, whereas the small

'djammer' navigational transmitter. Blurred e caused by the speed close proximity of the aft in a particularly daring ation. Notice turntable ierial array.

nt Würzburg (sometimes d a basket). Close up with rman operator watching RU aircraft.

wo 'Freya' radar lations near Audeville. ierial array was actually on the stereo ographs, to be moving.

Würzburg paraboloids were mobile. Their duties lay in the detection of aircraft in conjunction with the Freyas, but because of the movement of the bowl swivelling about on its axis, they were able to determine the height of approaching enemy aircraft. These small Würzburgs were sometimes used for flak and searchlight control, and occasionally for ship watching.

The Giant Würzburgs were vast, the bowl being about 24 feet in diameter, and the first one was originally described by a visitor to Berlin in 1941. It was said that the enormous bowl was not made of metal, but of a sort of lattice mesh forming a framework, and defended by a flak gun on a tower.

During December 1941, two sections of the searchlight belt protecting NW Germany, were established in Belgium from Bree in the north to Riezes in the south, and in front of this belt at intervals of 10 kilometres were clusters of three searchlight emplacements. Suddenly, between 3rd and 5th May 1942, it was seen that the whole of the searchlight belt had been evacuated, but the three searchlight clusters remained.

A sortie was flown over an area east of Brussels which included a German night fighter airfield at St Trond, and at about five miles from the airfield, photographs showed a Giant Würzburg sitting in the middle of three emplaced searchlights with another Giant sited a little distance away from them. They were also accompanied by a Freya.

The installations acted as control for German night fighters on what was known as the Kammhuber Belt operating in defence against Allied attacks in the Fatherland. They were in no way connected with searchlight control as was thought previously. A very large number of the Würzburgs were identified by Wavell's team.

Another exciting discovery by the team was that of several Giants lying about outside workshops of the Zeppelin factory at Friedrichshafen in the summer of 1943. The photographs found their way to the Radar Section by chance again, and this important news was flashed to Air Ministry, resulting in the bombing attack on 22nd June 1943 when the whole enormous plant was reduced to rubble.

Other types of RDF installations gradually made their appearance on the interpretation scene, all causing a deal of head scratching when they were first seen on photographs. They were known from their appearance as Chimneys and Hoardings, Pole Freyas and Limber Freyas, and then Benitos and Coastwatchers.

ADI(Sc) helped with the information to clear up the mysteries.

One of the major commitments of the section at Medmenham in early 1944, was the compilation, production and issue of 'Rhubarb Operations Appendix XII', which planned for the rapid and complete destruction of the enemy's radar warning systems during the two weeks immediately preceding D-day, and on which so much depended for the success or failure of the invasion.

Squadron Leader Wavell and his team were responsible for the complete target material required for briefing air crews for attacks on nearly a hundred separate radar, navigational beam and radar jamming stations, over an area bounded by the north coast of France to a depth of twenty miles. The production ran to 253 bound copies of over 300 pages which included descriptions, photographs and plans showing the relation of each piece of apparatus to its headquarters, with flak and other defences. Because of the Top Secret classification, all collating and binding was undertaken by members of the section.

The publication of the Appendix contributed in no small way to the success of Operation Overlord, as the majority of radar installations were destroyed by rocket-firing Typhoons and fighter aircraft, enabling the invasion fleets to rendezvous and attain their objectives without being detected by enemy radar. During the actual period of the preparatory attacks, and in spite of the appalling difficulties and danger the pilots experienced in obtaining the photographs, damage assessment reports from the Radar Section were issued only a few hours after each attack. In this way a complete photographic record of the progress of the operation was obtained, showing the measure of destruction as it occurred.


One of Claude Wavell's personal folders is full of information regarding his 'Altazimeter', an invention which proved of great value to the members of his section and elsewhere.

The need for determining the height of masts supporting aerial arrays arose when it became one of the essential features to be included in all interpretation reports on W/T – essential as a factor in the assessment of the capability of an instrument. It was a time-consuming task, taking sometimes thirty minutes to complete by the usual conventional computations, and was extremely tedious. Accordingly when Squadron Leader Wavell placed his brain-child, the Altazimeter, before his team, it was regarded with much

(*Left*) Portrait of the Altazimeter, Squadron Leader Wavell's brain child.

(*Below*) Squadron Leader Claude Wavell and Flight Lieutenant Eric Goodwin in the Radar Section.

approval and admiration, as it reduced the calculations to a question of minutes.

The essential data for operating the Altazimeter were: the latitude of the installation obtained from the map; azimuth of the sun (the declination of the sun in relation to the celestial equator either north or south); the photographic scale, and the length of the shadow of the mast.

The prototype Altazimeter was constructed of a number of narrow circles of plywood which fitted and slid over one another, and was put together by Claude himself. The circles were of three different diameters, and after being positioned, made three skeleton spheres one inside the other; the ultimate form being virtually a model of the celestial sphere with the earth as its centre. The inventor made this comment: 'Crude as the instrument as such appears to be, comparative results to date are well within 1% of those obtained with computation, and certainly within the accuracy of the data fed into it.'

Finally, feeling that perhaps he should have received some recognition for the success of his invention, Squadron Leader Wavell applied to Air Ministry and spent many years trying to satisfy questions as to proof of its usefulness. A cheque for £25 was the result.

### *A SONNET ON A SPHEROID*

O wondrous spheroid gadget, now complete  
With scales and whatnots properly adjusted;  
Designed to help when e'er the brain with heat  
From calculating heights is nearly busted;  
For many moons within a dusty niche  
The cabinet surmounting, all agog  
To start thy multifarious duties, which  
Appear to be dependent on the log;  
To any uninitiated reader  
The scales thou bearest seem as clear as mud –  
But, scanned with rapture by the Squadron Leader,  
They bring hard facts to light, as from the bud  
A rose comes forth to bloom in all its glory.  
And here, I think, I'd better end my story.

[G.A. Feltham]

# CHAPTER THIRTEEN

# Sinister Weapons
## V-1s, V-2s and, worse, V-3s

The threat of the German Vergeltungswaffen (revenge weapons), or as they were generally known in this country, the V-1 flying bomb, doodle bug or buzz bomb, the V-2 long-range rocket or German A-4, and the V-3 mystery weapons which fortunately for London and Bristol never became operational, has been well documented in other publications, but how the story unfolded through the stereos of the interpreters is less well known.

The first hint of Hitler's secret weapons reached Medmenham in January 1943, followed by a directive from MI14 War Office in February the following month, to the effect that the Germans were developing some form of long-range projectile capable of firing on England from the French coast. The information was meagre and the only concrete evidence was that the projector might resemble a section of railway track. The interpreters were requested to keep a close watch on suspicious erections such as rails or scaffolding.

Later, in March 1943, MI14 added specifications of possible range, weight and dimensions; also that the obvious target for such a weapon would be London. That part of France within a radius of 130 miles had to be watched. The directive added that reports had been received stating that the Wolfgaast-Peenemünde area of Germany, south of Rugen Island in the Baltic, was being used for experiments on the weapon.

Towards the end of March 1943 a PI report was received by MI14 describing three large emplacements seen on the latest sortie over Peenemünde. These consisted of three oval earthbanks, not unlike empty reservoirs, and in the centre of each were scaffoldings straddling a concrete slit in the ground. The report stated that it had not been possible to determine the nature of these workings, but that they were being actively developed.

Tardily, on 19th April 1943, Air Ministry issued an edited version of the directive, instructing the interpreters to begin an investigation into the enemy's secret weaponry as a whole, and to report, not only to Air Ministry and the War Office, but to Duncan

Sandys (then Minister of Supply) who was now appointed as co-ordinator of all the evidence from whatever source, as to the existence of a long-range rocket.

The directive was, if anything, even more vague than that of the War Office, as no specifications were given, and only a few suggestions as to the nature of the weapon were included. It was thought that it might be a long-range gun, a rocket-controlled aircraft on the Queen Bee principle, or some sort of tube located in a disused mine out of which a rocket could be squirted.

What amounted to a phenomenally heavy burden was then laid on the shoulders of the Photographic Reconnaissance Units and the CIU by a request in the Air Ministry directive that areas within 130 miles of London and 130 miles of Southampton were to be scrutinised, using photographs taken not earlier than January 1943, and all gaps in the flying were to be made up immediately by arranging additional flights. The following day saw the start of this arduous programme, the flying being shared by both the RAF and the USAAF Photographic Reconnaissance Squadrons.

It is not difficult to imagine the reactions of officers in charge of sections at Medmenham when reading such unenlightening briefing – it was almost as unhelpful as telling a blind man to cross the road without a stick. Those approached who might have been likely to come across some sort of tube located in a disused mine from which a rocket could be squirted, or a long-range gun located anywhere, must have thought they were being manipulated by agents from another world.

Wing Commander Kendall instructed Squadron Leader Hamshaw-Thomas (for the RAF) and his opposite Army number Major Norman Falcon, to set up two sub-sections. The RAF sub-section was in the charge of Flight Lieutenant André Kenny who, with his team, was responsible for the investigations for the Peenemünde area, while for the Army Captain Robert Rowell and his team dealt with that of Northern France. So far as the Sandys enquiry was concerned, the whole emphasis was on Peenemünde as those officers in the know at Medmenham soon discovered, when a group of engineers and scientists of the Ministry of Supply visited the unit on 24th April 1943.

As a result of suggestions from the MOS group and from photographic evidence, Duncan Sandys reached the conclusion that a heavy long-range rocket was not then an immediate menace, but that the frequent sorties to photograph the Peenemünde establishment were to be continued.

Then came a shock. In mid-May 1943, a large concrete structure was discovered near Watten in the Pas de Calais on a sortie flown by one of the PR units. It was a mystery and it could not be connected with any known military objective, as the Army team under Captain Rowell were in a position to affirm.

Almost at the same time, hundreds of miles away at Peenemünde, came more alarming news. One of the regular sorties flown over the experimental establishment revealed, in addition to the general frenetic activity, that a railway flat wagon had been loaded with a cylindrical object projecting over the following flat, approximately 38 feet by 6 feet. Another of these objects was seen on a second sortie.

The information was sufficient for Duncan Sandys to notify the War Cabinet that the existence of a long-range rocket could be confirmed, and indeed already might be in limited production.

The scientists taking part in the V-2 rocket investigation had already divided themselves into two factions over the months, and at this point, bitter controversy broke out – a controversy that was to continue until the first V-2 landed on London; the enormous explosion then being described as that caused by a broken gas main to allay fears. One faction was headed by Lord Cherwell, (Paymaster General and personal scientific adviser to the Prime Minister), who would have none of the rocket project, arguing that it was not feasible due to the problems of existing propellants. He maintained that the fat white shapes seen on the railway flats were in all probability barrage balloons. The leader of the opposition, Dr R.V. Jones, head of ADI(Sc), contended that rockets could and would be fired against England.

The activity on the site of Peenemünde consisted of constructional work within the oval emplacements, with traverser cranes wandering about inside them, and various buildings under construction adjacent to them. The vast complex included two factories, various workhops, a power station, and a light railway. A very large area to the north had been put aside for the aircraft factory airfield used for prototype testing, where the Me163 was soon to be identified by the Medmenham aircraft section in June 1943. An additional large slice of the complex was used for personnel accommodation.

The team under Flight Lieutenant Kenny came to the conclusion in April 1943 that the earthworks area might have something to do with rocket launching pads, and a later sortie confirmed the opinion that rockets were to be fired from the site. The first of a stereo pair showed a flame emerging from a test bed on which a rocket motor must have been installed horizontally, while on the second print there was no sign of flame. The prints were shown to General Smuts who was a regular visitor to Medmenham, and André Kenny remembers saying to him that in his view this was a visible and credible proof of rocketry.

The next excitement occurred when the sortie of 12th June 1943 was received at Medmenham and the prints passed to the Kenny team. A strange-looking object was discovered on the fan-shaped foreshore. It was standing upright and was described in the subsequent report as 'a vertical column about 40 feet high and 4 feet thick'.

It must be stressed once again that interpretation officers were not permitted to make definitive statements about any object they might have seen on photographs until it had been established by the authorities for what it was in actual terms, no matter what the PIs might have deduced personally. André Kenny, who had the misfortune to describe the mysterious things he saw at Peenemünde as either an object or a vertical column according to the rules laid down by his superior officers, has been pilloried by almost every writer on the subject for not spelling out the word 'rocket'. A scientist, for instance, implies that the CIU interpreters failed in their duty to identify the rocket, and that he was responsible for the discovery.[1] André Kenny, on the other hand, assures me that none of the highly trained PIs who had studied the photographs ever doubted that the objects were rockets. In any event, Wing Commander Kendall and his teams are to be congratulated for arriving at the solution without the advantages of the additional information available to others.

As a result of the exciting sortie of 12th June and a subsequent one of brilliant quality on 28th June 1943, Duncan Sandys reported to the Defence Committee in order to give his reasons for being convinced that the existence of the V-2 rocket was fact, and that a full scale raid should be mounted against Peenemünde as soon as possible. The CIU model section had been brought into the action and on 11th July 1943 had produced a scale model of the 'vertical column' with its attending vehicles at foot and a fine representation of the buildings in and around one of the oval emplacements. A

[1] *Most Secret War*. Professor Dr R.V. Jones, Hamish Hamilton, 1978.

second model of one of the rockets seen lying horizontally in the open was completed for the benefit of Duncan Sandys who wished to know how various conclusions as regards shape had been reached. Both were used in briefing the subsequent raid.

A version of the Duncan Sandys' summary reached CIU and Douglas Kendall, including in it the statement that having regard to the size of the projectiles the projector sites would be rail-served, unidentified installations having been discovered in northern France, notably at Wizernes, Marquise and Watten, which were all rail-served. This assumption turned out to be inaccurate as it was learnt later that the rocket was capable of travelling anywhere on special motor vehicles (*Meillerwagen*) and could be fired from almost any flat surface.

It was at this time that the code name 'Bodyline' was given to the V-weapon investigation, some humorist having selected the name for the term bodyline bowling, which in cricketing parlance, was not only against the rules but certainly unsportsmanlike.

The attack on Peenemünde took place on 17th/18th August 1943 and had to be carried out from the very low altitude of 8,000 feet. Bomber crews were advised of the great importance of the target, and were asked to accept any risk in order to destroy or seriously damage it. Forty heavy bombers were lost that night involving nearly 300 airmen. Not all were killed and many ended up in prisoner-of-war camps.

On 19th August 1943 the weather was clear and photographs showed that the attack had been successful, a number of permanent buildings being destroyed. Later it was revealed that development and testing were seriously disrupted and the whole project was set back by several months. Key personnel, including one of the chief designers, Dr Thiel, were killed.

In March 1944 reliable ground intelligence reports reached Air Ministry to the effect that activity on a large scale had been noticed at an artillery range near the village of Blizna in eastern Poland not far from the Russian frontier. Aerial torpedoes were being fired from the site, they said. The locality was well out of range of PR aircraft based in Britain, and so to investigate this further alarming news the first sortie was flown from San Severo in Italy on 15th April 1944 by a Mosquito which had to cover 900 miles to obtain the photographs. Nothing relating to V-2s was found, but a flying bomb ramp was identified; the first of these ramps had already been identified at Peenemünde on a sortie flown on 28th November

V-2 Rockets at Peenemünde (*Below*) Three rockets (A) in vertical position ready for firing. One is surrounded by fuelling and servicing vehicles (B) and there are several trailers (C). The area inside the dotted line was reclaimed from the Baltic for firing experiments. (*Inset*) A June 1943 photograph showing two rockets (A) lying horizontally inside the elliptical earthwork; rocket trailers (B) and roof flak (C).

(*Bottom photograph*) Model made at CIU of the then unknown weapon from information obtained from photographs.

1943 and the story is told in the next section on the V-1s. A second sortie on 5th May 1944 over Blizna revealed a rocket lying in the open, and this time it could be established that it had four fins. However, what puzzled the interpreters and caused consternation at Air Ministry Intelligence was the fact that no earthworks were seen. This meant that no one seemed any nearer to solving the mystery of launching.

In May 1944 firm evidence of the existence of the rocket reached Air Ministry Intelligence that on the 20th a V-2 had fallen into the River Bug near the village of Sarnaki, NW of Warsaw. The missile had malfunctioned and was lying in the water with its fins showing. Polish patriots of the underground movement rushed to the spot, reaching it before the Germans, and with great skill and heroism, dismantled the thing and somehow smuggled the bits to Warsaw where a Polish professor examined it. They were finally placed in the middle of a field and picked up by the pilot of a Dakota on a very daring mission.

About a month later, on 13th June 1944, a second rocket launched from Peenemünde malfunctioned, and exploded in mid-air over Sweden. British RAF officers were able to examine the pieces, and when the report of the findings was issued from ADI(Sc), it included the very important statement from a prisoner-of-war, that the rocket could be launched from a simple concrete slab.[1]

No news of this vital intelligence reached Medmenham at any stage of the investigation, and, according to Douglas Kendall who was, after all, the Wing Commander in charge of operations at ACIU, he and the team deduced from photographic evidence alone that the whole firing system of the V-2 was mobile and could be fired from any flat area. This was the beginning of August 1944, and they only learnt of the confirmation of their interpretation when Allied troops over-ran a launching area on the Island of Walcheren in November 1944.

Owing to the mobility of the rocket on the ground, it was obvious to the PIs that no firing sites could be confirmed from photographic evidence unless a rocket was actually seen in the process of fuelling and in the vertical position. It was not until after the first rocket had fallen on Chiswick on 8th September 1944 that two fresh clearings in woods at Rijs in Holland were noticed in October and November

---

[1] *The Secret War*, Brian Johnson BBC.

1944 in an area known, from radar plotting, to have been used for rocket launching. In a vain attempt to discover some clue which might lead to successful counter-measures, the interpreters were instructed to examine thousands upon thousands of photographs without any positive result. If the clues had been visible the interpreters would have found them.

Finally and ironically, on 26th February 1945, a V-2 rocket was photographed sitting proudly in a vertical position among its attendant vehicles on a rough road in a scattered wood at Duindigt near the Hague. It was photographed by three separate PR aircraft within five minutes of each other.

On 27th March 1945 the last V-2 was fired against England to fall at Orpington, so for nearly six months these frightening weapons spewed themselves over our country. One thousand one hundred and fifteen of them dived into the ground and exploded, and of these, five hundred and seventeen arrived in the London area. Two thousand and fifty-four citizens died, and six thousand seven hundred and twenty-three were seriously injured. Antwerp suffered even more from the rocket attacks.

## The V-1 Flying Bomb

On 28th October 1943 as a result of continual activity seen at the mysterious constructions in northern France, and from a directive from Duncan Sandys, the area within a 130 mile range of London was to be rephotographed. This was to be the third time that the whole area had been studied, and it entailed an enormous amount of flying effort at the large photographic scale of 1:10,000. Possibly a hundred or so separate sorties would have been necessary.

The Army interpreters specialising in the northern France Bodyline area, found themselves in the same position as their colleagues working on the Peenemünde establishment in that they had no real idea for what they were supposed to be looking because of the vagueness of their brief. They had been told that the object to be fired (presumably a rocket) was so heavy that rail access was essential. On that account, not very much time was given to searching areas away from the main railway lines.

At the beginning of November 1943 a message from a French agent arrived in London to the effect that his construction firm had been engaged by the Germans to build eight sites for an unknown purpose in northern France. The agent indicated the area and a sortie was flown. Sure enough, the interpreters were able to identify the eight sites under construction. They were being built to a pattern, concealed in woods, and significantly there was no rail access; they were only served by roads.

The first of the sites to be examined was at Bois Carré, from which all similar sites were to take the name, and as well as investigating the new sorties, the team set about retrieving all suitable former sorties covering the area, because so much had been left unexamined as a result of the erroneous brief that the sites had to be rail-served. By midnight 7th November 1943 no fewer than nineteen Bois Carré sites had been identified.

A meeting, presided over by Sir Stafford Cripps, whose duty it was to advise the War Cabinet on further steps to be taken regarding the V-weapon investigation, was convened for 8th November 1943 and Wing Commander Kendall, Captain Neil Simon and Flight Lieutenant André Kenny were requested to attend. It must have been an awe-inspiring occasion for them as the room was filled with very senior officers from various branches of intelligence, Mr Duncan Sandys and the eminent scientists.

Evidence from non-photographic sources was on the whole vague, and the rest of the meeting was given over to a detailed discussion of the photographic evidence regarding the V-2 – assuming there was one. At the end of the scientific arguments, Sir Stafford Cripps asked if there was any more information regarding the possible secret weapon activity in northern France. This was the moment for Douglas Kendall to get to his feet, faced with the unpalatable task of telling the meeting that nineteen sites in the early stages of development were under construction.

At this alarming news, Sir Stafford Cripps asked what evidence was there to show that these sites had any connection with Operation Bodyline, and Douglas replied that there was none of a positive nature, but there existed a considerable amount of negative evidence. He told his listeners that the sites did not correspond with any known military installation; construction of all nineteen was started simultaneously, and they appeared to have no connection with coastal defences. Furthermore, the sites had certain noticeable features in common; three ski-shaped buildings (so called from the appearance of a ski lying on its side) and a platform lined up in the direction of London. Douglas Kendall's bombshell caused such consternation that the meeting was adjourned for two days to give time for further examination of sorties. Obviously drastic changes in organisation had to be undertaken to cope with the sudden surge of requests for intelligence, so a sub-section was set up to deal with this particular facet of Operation Bodyline now named Crossbow. The new section was put in charge of Captain Robert Rowell with a majority of RAF and WAAF officers in the team, five or six army officers, and ORs from the Army, RAF and USAAF.

By the time the meeting was resumed, Kendall was in a position to advise Sir Stafford Cripps that ninety-six Bois Carré sites had been located, and amongst the constructional items could be seen the platforms aligned towards London, and of course the ski-shaped buildings. The Wing Commander was also able to report that in his opinion and that of his team, the ski-shaped buildings were intended for storage, and that from the general lay-out of the sites, there seemed to be no reason to assume that they could be used in the firing of rockets which were supposed to weigh 45 tons and would therefore need heavy handling gear. This statement refutes Professor R.V. Jones' claim that he had to convince the interpreters before they would disallow the rocket hypothesis.[1]

The function of these sites remained a mystery at that stage, and even the existence of the rocket was an arguable point over which the scientists were still locked in battle, and anything that looked remotely like a flying bomb, had not appeared on photographs. The thought of tubes out of which a rocket could be squirted, or rails, or scaffolding or perhaps a ramp, must have acted like some maddening, ceaseless merry-go-round of useless information. Nothing fitted and so much was at stake – possibly fearful destruction in the south of England, and possibly the adverse effect of the mystery weapons on the careful planning of Operation Overlord (the Allied invasion of north-west Europe).

Rumours began to reach the team, once the ninety-six sites had been discovered, that the number under construction might be as high as 400. More frenzied search over the same ground ensued with no result, which in reality made sense as the official German figures totalled ninety-six – the team had overlooked none.

The programme of photographic investigation was then worked out, the first stage being the search for features in common. Standard buildings seemed to be the most profitable study, as the layout varied only marginally from site to site. The operators of the Wild machine benefited as well, for it made it easy for them to produce completed plans of any sites nearing completion. In fact, it

[1] *Most Secret War*.

was not difficult to deduce the number of internal divisions of a building by the study of the walls before the roof would be added. One high-ranking army officer on a visit to Medmenham, while examining a model of one of the buildings, lifted its roof and asked, 'How on earth could you possibly know what was inside from just staring at photographs?'

The Crossbow team set about probing sortie after sortie on their voyage of discovery, and very gradually some sort of sense began to reveal itself. The three extraordinary-looking buildings shaped rather like skis lying on their sides and which could be seen on each site, were the most striking feature. Two would be of equal length; that is to say the straight part of the 'ski' would be in the order of 228 feet while the curved portion was 40 feet. The third ski building was always shorter, the straight portion being 196 feet with its curved end of 45 feet. Internally both width and height were $9\frac{1}{2}$ feet. There were no windows and the walls were approximately 3 feet thick of pre-cast concrete with a small door for personnel at the closed end of the curved portion. But why the curved piece? The team concluded finally that it was only designed as an anti-blast measure. Normally a blast wall would be erected in front of an entrance, but in this case, if long objects were being stored in the odd-shaped buildings, they would have been unable to pass the blast wall.

A concrete platform was another item of importance for the interpreters to chew over, and a great deal of information was extracted from it. It was made of a slab of heavily re-inforced concrete with a narrow sunken slit along the middle of it, and near the end nearest the centre of the site was a small building, also of concrete and sunk into the ground with only about one or two feet showing above it. In front of the other end of the platform were six pairs of concrete studs (each with a hole in it) about twenty feet apart sunk into the ground and in a line directed towards London.

The studs were an important clue as they indicated to the team that some type of steel support would be embedded into them, almost certainly to bear a ramp. As for the small building, in all probability it was intended for the use of some chap to press a button to launch or fire whatever it was.

This stage of the investigation having been reached, the deduction that some weapon was to be fired from a ramp inclined at a low angle, precluded any idea of a rocket which would assuredly dive straight into the ground. On the other hand, should the weapon be winged, it could be launched from a nearly horizontal position. Winged it would have to be – a pilotless aircraft or a flying bomb.

A square concrete building about 44 x 44 feet was always to be found fairly near the concrete platform with which it was always aligned for some odd reason. The entrance faced London, and owing to the fact that it was very wide (22 feet across) in proportion to the building, the overall appearance was similar to a small hangar. This was important news as thereby it seemed certain that due to the fact that the ski-buildings were too small to house a flying bomb with wings attached, this hangar-type building was certainly the assembly point for the weapon to have its wings and things attached. However, this did not explain why the building had to be aligned to the concrete platform.

It did not take the interpreters very long to reach the conclusion that an automatic pilot was to be set in motion based on magnetics for direction. Then, at an unusually apposite moment, an intelligence report from Air Ministry was passed down to the team. A French agent employed by one of the building contractors, had stated that the Germans were meticulous with regard to the materials used in one of the buildings which the Crossbow team could recognise as the hangar-type construction. It was to be made entirely of concrete with no metal parts whatsoever – even the door hinges were of some synthetic material. This evidence indicated that, as the interpreters had surmised, the flying bomb would be aligned to the magnetic heading it was briefed to fly on.

The almost fanatical German thoroughness in attempting to direct the V-1s accurately on target, caused some amusement at Medmenham as London is, after all an immense area, and wind conditions could not be accurately forecast. French maps of the Napoleonic era were not based on the geodetic system of the United Kingdom, so accordingly the engineers of the German Army were given the colossal task of making a completely new geodetic survey by taking observations across the Straits of Dover. CIU was perfectly aware of what was going on because, to use Douglas Kendall's own words: 'It was actually easier than it sounds as the Germans employed a standard type of geodetic tower which we christened "spires" and which was used for the taking of instrument observations; and could with a little care be identified on photographs. Then by plotting each one observed, the geodetic pattern would emerge. I imagine the bearing of each firing ramp was tied into the revised geodetic points with great precision.'

A sunken 'T' shaped building well protected against blast was viewed with interest as it could only mean the storage of fuel. No-one had been told of the type required for the launching of the V-1, although hydrogen peroxyde with sodium permanganate was known by ADI(Sc) to be the activating force in the first stage of the launch; nor were they informed that a piston carrying the V-1 with it would charge up the ramp, disengage itself at the top, and end up on the ground some distance after the pulsating weapon had lifted off to the skies away from the launching ramp. Only after the sites had become operational were the Crossbow team able to deduce that a piston was being used by seeing skid marks on the ground, and from their former observations in discovering a slot in the concrete platform to guide the path of the piston. They were also able to calculate how often a site was being operated by counting not only the skid marks of the pistons, but the craters left by V-1s malfunctioning and exploding on the ground.

The complicated system of concreted tracks told almost the whole story of the movement of the components of the V-1s from the point of arrival by road, through to fuelling points and where its explosive head might be added if it had not already been fitted, and compressed air pumped into it. The fuselages and wings would be trundled about on separate trolleys (as there were no turning points for tractors) and taken to the ski-shaped buildings for storage; large ones to house fuselages and the smaller ones for wings. Near the firing time, more trundling of complete sets of wings and fuselages to the square building for assembly and setting up of the automatic pilots would follow, and then finally another journey for the completed flying bomb to the firing point at the bottom of the ramp.

By the time the team had examined all the buildings, installations and electric power cables on the sites they had a good idea of what type and capability of weapon they were to expect; although none had yet seen it.

### The Flying Bomb discovered

The most logical step to take in November 1943 was to try and find a winged object of about 20 feet wingspan, possibly to be seen at some place of manufacturing or testing; and a launching ramp would have to be somewhere. Considering the vast areas where these relatively minute objects could be located, the task to the

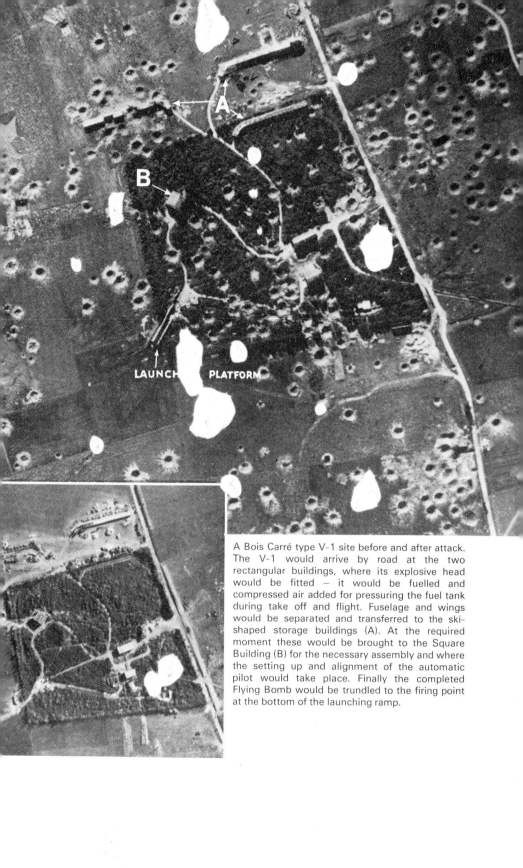

A Bois Carré type V-1 site before and after attack. The V-1 would arrive by road at the two rectangular buildings, where its explosive head would be fitted — it would be fuelled and compressed air added for pressuring the fuel tank during take off and flight. Fuselage and wings would be separated and transferred to the ski-shaped storage buildings (A). At the required moment these would be brought to the Square Building (B) for the necessary assembly and where the setting up and alignment of the automatic pilot would take place. Finally the completed Flying Bomb would be trundled to the firing point at the bottom of the launching ramp.

uninitiated might seem impossible.

Douglas Kendall decided that the Aircraft Section (Constance Babington Smith and her team) were the obvious people to turn to, and gave them a firm brief to search for a very small aeroplane of about 20 feet wingspan. The sortie covering Peenemünde on 23rd June 1943 was retrieved from the print library, and sure enough something suspiciously like a small aircraft was spotted, not on the airfield, but behind a hangar. However definition was so poor that the evidence was not sufficient for confirmation.

The search continued through old sorties and it was quite by chance at the beginning of December 1943 when the first clue was discovered by the Aircraft Section near a group of installations used for reclamation purposes. It was an unusual-looking object, possibly some form of ramp pointing out to sea, and as the Industry Section was responsible for that area, they were dutifully consulted and said that the object was probably part of the reclamation machinery. Babs, being more flying-bomb-conscious than her colleagues in industry although she knew practically nothing about Crossbow at that stage, notified Wing Commander Kendall who, almost at once, recognised the mysterious shape for what it was; the missing launching ramp for fitting onto those concrete studs seen on the Bois Carré sites.

The officer-in-charge of the sub-section dealing with the rocket investigations at Peenemünde and elsewhere has received a hammering from several authors, including Professor Jones, who state that the launching ramp was misinterpreted as a 'sludge-pump'. To put the record straight I contacted André Kenny who assured me that the allegation was incorrect. In his capacity as a land-drainage expert, a much earlier sortie covering the area was brought to him for his comments, and he was able to identify suction dredgers but did not apply this term to what later turned out to be the launching ramp. These findings were supported by his senior officer Squadron Leader Hamshaw-Thomas, and had nothing in common with a ramp seen on the later sortie.

While the aircraft section was immersing itself in old cover of Peenemünde, a Mosquito took off from Scotland on 28th November 1943 on a mission to photograph Berlin. Cloud covered the city so the pilot turned north to cover secondary targets on the Baltic coast including Peenemünde. When the prints were examined by the section, the same ramp was noticed on the very first single print without its stereo pair. Even so it was clear that an object was sitting on it – an object which everyone from the Prime Minister down had been waiting for and dreading – the V-1 Flying bomb, and this was the first identification of this beautifully designed evil piece of military hardware.

The same sortie produced rich gleanings; further information for Claude Wavell's radar section, and a windfall for Robert Rowell and Neil Simon with their Crossbow team. For the first time, a prototype launching site, exactly similar to those seen in northern France, but minus the ski-shaped storage buildings, was discovered between Zinnowitz and the village of Zempin on the Peenemünde peninsula.

Moments such as these compensated for hours, days, months of fruitless searching. The photograph of the V-1 was obtained in November 1943, and it was reasonable for the team to assume that the prototype had not been completed until August when construction of the Bois Carré sites had begun. This development was calculated on the evidence obtained from photographic intelligence uniquely, and as Douglas Kendall pointed out: 'It was not difficult to visualise what sort of position we would have been in without it as a source.'

There was still a certain amount of mystification as to the reason why no launching sites had been found in Germany. With the available knowledge of German thoroughness, it seemed inconceivable that there might not be a prototype somewhere in that country. Sure enough, three months later, three firing ramps were discovered in a military training camp on the east Baltic coast near Königsberg. One single ski unit, a rectangular building and two square buildings were shared by three firing ramps. To everyone's delight there had just been a malfunction when the photograph had been taken, resulting in the top end of a ramp being blown to smithereens.

The next problem was to develop some method of assessing the priorities required for successful bomb attacks against individual sites. All that was known so far was that they would become operational within 120 to 140 days from the start of construction, and that 96 sites had to be considered.

Kendall and the boys and girls of the Crossbow team produced a brilliant 'marks' system between them. The main components on a site were each awarded points according to their importance; the total for a site equally 100 points. As new sorties covering the area were examined, each item was re-assessed and points added according to progress. When the total reached 70 (or 70%), the moment had come to pass on the information that the site should be included in the next bomber hit-list.

Weather conditions which might have prevented reconnaissance had to be taken into consideration as well; so on the basis that a site would take 120 to 140 days to complete, each day was allotted $\frac{3}{4}$ point. Given that a site had reached 65 points, the number of day-points would bring the total to 70 when it would automatically be placed on the bombing list even though it might not have been possible to photograph it each day.

Damage to sites could also be included in the system, as points would be deducted accordingly thereby altering the position in priority bombing.

| | |
|---|---:|
| 3 skis at 10 points | 30 points |
| Square Building | 10 points |
| 2 Rectangular buildings at 8 points | 16 points |
| Launching platform | 10 points |
| Sunken building | 5 points |
| Water hole | 5 points |
| Path system | 15 points |
| Other installations | 9 points |
| | Total 100 points |

The locality of the supply bases for the Bois Carré sites was of equal importance and these were placed high in bombing priorities, and following the usual procedure of carefully amassing all available photographic evidence, it became possible for the team to deduce that a total of eight supply depots would each be centrally placed vis-à-vis twelve launching sites, which totalled the 96 already plotted; the supplies would be contained in buildings rather similar to those of ammunition dumps and would be rail-served. This deduction was proved correct.

By March 1944 all the known Bois Carré sites had been heavily bombed, and those nearing completion destroyed. This was no time for self-congratulation, however, as unknown to the interpreters, a new type of launching ramp was being developed to take their place – and suddenly the Crossbow team came across it, much to everyone's disquiet. The new site was discovered near Belhamelin and was thenceforth to be known by that name or a 'Modified' site, as were others of the same type.

The Belhamelins were a sort of poor relation to the Bois Carrés,

Flight Officer Nora Littlejohn, a leading member of the Crossbow team, pointing to a
V-1 on the launching ramp at a Belhamelin site.

and fiendishly difficult to detect in their early days. Only the familiar ramp and the foundations of the square building and one other building were visible; there were no servicing or storage facilities and what could be identified were carefully concealed beneath trees or near farm buildings. At first glance the sites looked as if they had been abandoned, but it became clearly evident when buildings started going up, that all the installations were pre-fabricated, and that the V-1 would have to arrive on site complete with fuel and compressed air.

This method of construction gave the interpreters an accurate forecast of things to come. From the moment that the ramp was installed, the calculation could be made for that particular site to become operational within 24 or 48 hours. The team predicted accurately, that in the early hours of 13th June 1944 V-1s would be launched against London.

The phenomenal success of CIU in discovering all the Bois Carré sites was not to be repeated in the case of the Belhamelins. In May 1944 the Normandy landings were only about a month distant, therefore it was necessary virtually to switch the whole of the reconnaissance effort to essential targets in preparation for Operation Overlord, therefore bombing attacks on the V-1 sites had to be decreased in order to fulfil these new commitments. As a result, the interpreters had to face the added burden of examining hundreds of previous sorties (new cover not being available) and only twelve of the Belhamelins had been discovered by 3rd May 1944. It was not until the first flying bomb had been launched against London that the total number of 156 new-type sites had been discovered.

The damage and loss of life in the London area and elsewhere would have been inestimably worse if the enemy had not been forced to abandon the original Bois Carrés for inefficient installations which were not capable of rapid fire. A maximum of 300 V-1s launched in 24 hours was achieved from the Belhamelins, whereas the planned objective for the Bois Carré sites was 2,000 flying bombs for the same period.

Once again another search was on, this time for supply depots for the new sites. The Crossbow team could only judge that they would be smaller than the previous ones; in reasonable numbers, and would be receiving a continual supply from some main base, probably out of harm's way near Paris. Reports from agents established the existence of two underground storage depots near

Paris. They were confirmed by photographs, and both were attacked in July 1944 resulting in an immediate falling off in flying-bomb launches.

The most important discovery of all was a large underground factory in the Hartz Mountains near Niedersachwerfen, and by an incredible stroke of luck, railway flats conveniently left in the open were seen loaded with 'cylindrical objects'. Subsequently it was learnt that the factory was the sole source of supply of the V-weapons.

Perhaps it might not be out of place to recount my own experiences of being on the receiving end of a flying bomb.

I had been posted to AI3(c)1 to work on airfield targets, and our temporary office was on one of the upper floors of Lansdowne House, Berkeley Square, London, W1, overlooking Berkeley Street. One Sunday morning in August 1944 I had left my flat in Baker Street and had walked through steady rain to Lansdowne House. An air raid alert had been in force for several hours, but as we were a service establishment, we followed the usual procedure by remaining at our desks until special internal bells warned us that we should move away from windows as flying bomb attacks were becoming uncomfortably close. They rang, and each of us grabbed a cup of coffee and withdrew to the passage, forming a small group outside each office door. Being Sunday, there were very few of us there which was a mercy.

Innumerable explosions occurred outside, and one could see through the open office doors revolting-looking puffs of yellow smoke rising above the skyline after each one, and after a bit I left my particular group of colleagues and wandered away down the passage for another view. I had only walked a very short distance, when I noticed the office cat, a nice little black thing, tearing towards me like a maniac with ears back and fur standing on end. She shot past me, and at that very moment we were hit. She must have realised, from her feline second sight that something was going to happen, but received the wrong directional brief. I was the lucky one.

I had no sensation of noise, which seemed most peculiar as the flying bomb had driven itself into the roof immediately above us and exploded – all I was aware of was a swaying movement around me, dust rising everywhere, and a feeling of utter desolation and disorientation as many of the dividing walls had collapsed. I turned round to see what had happened to my friends and was horrified to be faced with a pile of rubble blocking the passage between us from floor to ceiling. Five of our personnel had been killed and several injured, as I learnt later. I was too stunned to move, and too stunned to answer the many questions plied to me by a group of air raid wardens and ambulance men who had materialised from a staircase which I never knew existed until the door had been blown off. One of the rescuers handed me an American officer's raincoat, and pushing me towards the staircase, said kindly: 'You're not needed here, love, get on your way home,' and I found myself walking towards Berkeley Square with the rain still pouring down.

Suddenly I was stopped by a young Naval officer, RNVR, brandishing a piece of sodden paper. It had TOP SECRET written all over it, and he asked me: 'Does this belong to you by any chance? It came floating down from somewhere.' I replied with something unintelligible and he looked at me closely. 'You look as if you need salvaging, come with me,' and taking my arm led me towards Charles Street. We came to the American Officers' Club of which he was a member, and where I had once disgraced myself by mistaking peanut butter for mustard.

My new friend addressed himself to a very elegant receptionist who was eyeing me with obvious disapproval. 'Is there anywhere for this officer (meaning me) to clean herself up?' he asked. My uniform was concealed under the raincoat filthy with plaster and brickdust, my hair also filthy, with streaks of the stuff all over my face and hands – I was a mess.

The elegant receptionist now stared at me with obvious distaste, and being English, behaved as if she were totally unaware of the mayhem that had been created just down the street. 'Are you a member?' she enquired loftily.

## Worse – the V-3s

It will be recalled that in May 1943 the attention of the interpreters was drawn to some sort of major constructional activity taking place in the Pas de Calais area of northern France. Very large concrete structures in the early stages of building showed up on the photographs, and no one had the faintest idea of their function at that stage. There was a vague notion at Medmenham that they might be connected with unknown V-nasties – probably those capable of squirting something out of the ground. As it turned out, that assumption was not very far from the truth in one case. All that the PIs had to work on was that the sites resembled nothing which could be bracketed with normal military installations, and that they were all rail-served. Information was so scanty that, in order to complete the picture of the V-weapons, although not from interpretation reports, I am including some of the findings of the Sanders Mission which was published in 1945.[1]

After D-day in the autumn of 1944, a mission was formed under Colonel T.R.B. Sanders of the Armament Design Department of the Ministry of Supply, at the request of Mr Duncan Sandys so that he could prepare a report for the Prime Minister, and on behalf of the Rocket Sub-Committee of Crossbow. The brief was to investigate the Crossbow installations then in Allied hands, or, as they were known, the 'Heavy Sites' so-called from the extent of the major constructional works.

The report issued in February 1945 is a remarkable document, drawing as it does from the opinions of officers from Air Ministry (including Squadron Leader André Kenny posted from CIU to AI1(h), the War Office, 21st Army Group, RAF Medmenham, and three French scientists.

Watten, near the main Calais-St Omer railway, was the first site to have been reported by CIU in May 1943, and heavy raids destroyed the early constructions in August and September 1943. Despite this set-back, more robust buildings began to take their place, and great activity was noticed right up to July 1944 when it was abandoned. Although it had been originally destined for a rocket launching point, by the time the members of the Mission had reached the site there was no sign that it was used for anything of an offensive nature, as all remaining evidence pointed to the production of hydrogen-peroxyde which was employed during the first stage of launching the flying bomb.

The site near Wizernes, constructed deep into a hillside close to the St Omer-Boulogne railway, was a most intriguing and futuristically planned project. It first appeared on photographs in August 1943, and similarly to Watten, despite heavy bombing, activity underground continued until it was abandoned in July 1943. The Sanders team at first hand discovered that vast underground workings had been under construction, and the intention seemed to them to have been the future firing of very large projectiles such as the V-2s, and they concluded that it would have

[1] WO 106/2817.

been possible to handle an even larger rocket of almost twice the size.

Dr Winifred Bartindale, when a WAAF officer at Medmenham, recalls seeing photographs of 'cylindrical objects' on railway flats somewhere in Poland. She maintains that they were very much larger than any of the rockets previously identified on photographs, and this evidence is interesting for it confirms the existence of the larger rockets mentioned in the Sanders Report.

Marquise/Mimoyecques was the fascinating name given to what was the most frightening in concept of all the Heavy Sites. At Medmenham in 1943 André Kenny was the first to notice that one haystack among others on a chalk hill close to the Calais-Boulogne railway, had suffered either from the effects of a gale-force wind or had been attacked by an over-enthusiastic fighter pilot. The haystack had disintegrated revealing a windlass and pulley at the top of a shaft for all the world to see. On subsequent sorties it was noticed that other haystacks were showing an inclination to move around in a mysterious fashion. At the same time, construction on two tunnels began, one into the side of the hill with the haystacks, and the other in the neighbouring hill to the west. The western site was abandoned after initial bombing in September 1943, and direct hits from Tallboy bombs in July 1944 caused the rest of the site to follow suit.

The two sites were originally intended to house fifty long-range guns in deep inclined shafts, twenty-five inserted into each hill. The barrels were to be approximately 400 feet long with a projectile in the order of 6 inches calibre weighing 120 lbs and containing 40 lbs of high explosive, and five barrels could be accommodated in each shaft with the associated firing chambers below. A system of lifts was to be installed for the handling of the projectiles and charges, and to give access to the breech chambers. The rate of fire was to be 5 rounds of 25 barrels every five minutes (by the time you had hard-boiled your egg, 125 shells each carrying 40 lbs of high explosive might with luck have passed over your house in England without stopping, at a velocity of 5,500 feet per second.)

The sites at Siracourt and Lottinghem were similar to each other in construction and were undoubtedly intended for the storage, assembly and launching of V-1s, while at Hidrequent, quarries were to be used for orthodox long-range railway guns.

The Mission recommended that both Marquise and Wizernes should be demolished, as in 1944 it was feared that in the event of

Siracourt. 'Heavy' site intended for storage, assembly and launching of V-1s.
showing the extent of bomb damage.

the sites being re-captured, they might be turned against England; so demolished they were and all tunnels sealed. It is difficult not to speculate on the inference that an archaeologist of the future might draw at the discovery of the remains, not only of the internal workings of the sites, but of the unfortunate French and Italian workers trapped under Marquise after the great bombs had been dropped. Nor should one give too much thought to the effect that the V-3 shells zooming up from the rapid firing long-range guns in their shafts in the hill, and a possible larger edition of the V-2 rocket, as well as the flying bombs, might have had on the already battered England of World War Two. It is almost too horrible to contemplate.

# Tail Piece

From a total of 206 (116 RAF and WAAF officers, 1 Army officer, no Naval officers, and 89 civilians) in 1940, the number of personnel rose at Medmenham to a maximum of 1,715 in 1944 (1,400 RAF and WAAF officers and ORs, all civilians having been absorbed; 113 Army and ATS officers and ORs; 15 RN, RNVR, WRN officers and NCOs.

At VE-day in May 1945, some sections closed almost immediately, while others worked on such subjects as the Control Commission requirements in Germany, or plotting and recording captured German photographic material.

The title Allied Central Interpretation Unit was dropped when US personnel left in August 1945, in favour of its former name of Central Interpretation Unit.

After the Print Library had been wound up in 1946, thousands of films had to be destroyed as they could not be stored in safety, due to the fact that they were manufactured of nitrate-based celluloid which is subject to spontaneous combustion. Albums of valuable prints made up as a pictorial record of RAF Medmenham were rescued in the nick of time before being thrown on the bonfire.

In the same year, CIU left Medmenham for good to be installed at its satellite, Nuneham Park, becoming known as the Joint Air Reconnaissance Centre (JARIC) which moved to RAF Brampton in 1957. As for me, after VE-day I was sent on a course of Far Eastern PI, and looked forward to being posted to the Pentagon. However, VJ day was declared, which obviously cancelled out any such future, and although vaguely flattered at being asked to remain in some sort of PI capacity related to targets intelligence, I could hardly wait to get out of the uniform for the last time and return to my own photographic profession. Life in the Service during peace-time was certainly not for me.

# Appendix
## Photographic Interpretation Today

The skills gained by the photographic interpreters at Medmenham during the war have not been lost. The Royal Air Force recognises the value of the craft in its Photographic Interpretation Branch, which offers career prospects to the rank of Group Captain, and in the PI Trade for NCOs to WO. The Joint Air Reconnaissance Intelligence Centre (JARIC), at RAF Brampton in Huntingdonshire, is the main British photographic interpretation unit and is the direct descendant of the Central Interpretation Unit. In addition to JARIC, the RAF has several Reconnaissance Intelligence Centres (RICs) established with tactical reconnaissance squadrons in the United Kingdom, West Germany and elsewhere. The RICs exist to provide immediate, or first-phase, reports of potential enemy activity in their areas of responsibility whilst JARIC provides detailed, or third-phase, reports.

The photographic interpreters of today, known as 'imagery analysts', speak glibly of 'imagery', 'sensors', 'platforms', and 'exploitation'. In addition to conventional monochrome photography – which is still the mainstay of aerial reconnaissance – there is a variety of complementary imagery obtained by sensor systems mounted on various aerial platforms. For example, the British Army's 'Midge' – the AN/USD-501 Drone – is an unmanned, rocker-assisted vehicle which flies on a programmed course and returns to deliver semi-panoramic monochrome or colour photography, infra-red false colour photography or infra-red line-scan imagery. Similarly, supersonic jet reconnaissance aircraft mount pods containing optical cameras, line-scan and radar sensors which can provide monochrome colour or false-colour photography and imagery derived from infra-red line-scan or sideways looking reconnaissance radar.

Such sensors provide imagery coverage by day and night. Infra-red line-scan (IRLS) records the relative difference in radiometric temperature of objects, helping to locate vehicles and personnel even when camouflaged or at night, and has been employed to detect heat losses from buildings during energy conservation campaigns by the Department of the Environment. Sideways looking reconnaissance radar (SLRR) can detect the movement of ships and vehicles by night, or during bad weather, and can 'map' areas inaccessible to optical cameras. Infra-red false colour (IRFC) emphasises the chlorophyll content of growing vegetation and is particularly useful in detecting camouflaged targets – especially when covered by cut foliage which rapidly changes its chlorophyll valance. IRFC has also been used for pollution studies off the coasts and for monitoring the extent of crop disease.

The task of the imagery analyst is to exploit such imagery to the full. At a RIC, time is of the essence and exploitation is accomplished within thirty minutes of the return of the aircraft. To achieve this requirement, imagery analysts examine film negatives and only resort to positive prints when photographic illustrations are required to accompany a report. The more protracted third-phase exploitation is undertaken by the study of diapositive photography taken directly from negatives. Diapositives – which are similar to commercially processed transparencies for slides – offer better definition and permit greater magnification and, as rolled film, are easier to handle and store than loose prints. To examine rolled negatives and diapositives, the main tool of the imagery analyst is the multi-strand light table equipped with zoom stereo-microscopes and motorised film drives. Optical and electronic measuring and calculating equipments are extensively used in conjunction with the light tables to produce very accurate measurements.

Computerisation has been introduced to alleviate many of the mundane tasks previously associated with film handling and data retrieval. JARIC maintains the British Services' library of aerial photography and all new photography is micro-filmed whilst the relevant details of areas covered are entered into a computer. When photography of a particular location is required, the computer is interrogated with the latitude and longitude of the target and produces details of available cover. The micro-film cassette indicated by the computer is viewed by a PI on a visual display unit and the required film is selected. The negative can then be withdrawn from the film library (the 'tin mines' familiar to veteran PIs) for reproduction or enlargement. Unfortunately, many of the war-time nitrate-based celluloid films became a storage hazard and were destroyed before copies could be made. Many of the mathematical formulae used for scaling, measuring and heighting objects on imagery have been computerised; progress control of tasks undertaken by JARIC is performed by computer as well as the recording of reference materials – which are available to PIs as microfiche viewed on display units.

JARIC remains a joint service unit with departments specialising in specific subjects – maritime, ground forces, aircraft, etc. The Royal Navy provides officer PIs, including members of the Women's Royal Naval Service, and the army provides officers and NCOs of the Intelligence Corps and the Womens Royal Army Corps. In addition to the regular forces, there is a trained and practiced reserve of volunteer PIs; the Royal Naval Reserve PI Group (which also includes WRNS), 21 Intelligence Company of the Intelligence and Security Group (Volunteers), Intelligence Corps, and 7010 Flight of the Royal Air Force Volunteer Reserve. Close liaison is maintained with the PIs of the USA, Canada and Australia, and PIs of NATO and other nations are trained at the Joint School of Photographic Interpretation at Royal Air Force Wyton. Throughout the NATO nations, the form and terminology of air reconnaissance reports are standardised and frequent tactical interoperability exercises familiarise NATO PIs with each others' equipment and methods. Thus, it is not unusual for a German PI to interpret imagery obtained by a RAF reconnaissance aircraft – and vice versa.

Despite technological advancements in the procuring and processing of imagery, the imagery analyst's role remains the same as it was in 1940: the examination of photographic images by the human eye (aided by optical and electronic devices) to extract items of intelligence value. However, it is not enough merely to recognise and locate a target – the 'what' and 'where'. Complete exploitation should also answer the 'who', 'how', and 'why'. The analyst must subject the imaged target to a 'dialectical evaluation', questioning the reasons for the presence of an object, comparing it with previous sightings and collateral information, considering its role, assessing its significance and potential. To answer these questions, the imagery analyst must have a good knowledge of the subject and must be aware of recent developments and the current situation. The analyst is an integral part of the intelligence organisation and is required to give briefings to both senior and junior staff. The value of photographic intelligence has become increasingly appreciated, not only by the intelligence staff at major headquarters but also by the troops on the ground.

Captain Hamish B. Eaton (Intelligence Corps)

# Glossary

| | |
|---|---|
| ACIU | Allied Central Interpretation Unit. |
| ADI(Ph) | Assistant Directorate Intelligence (Photographic) |
| ADI(Sc) | Assistant Directorate Intelligence (Science) |
| AHV | Armoured Heavy Vehicles |
| AI | Air Intelligence |
| AI1(h) | Department that took over AOC (qv) Wembley 1940 |
| AI2(b) | Air Intelligence German Airfields |
| AI2(c) | Air Intelligence Liaison SOE and RAF |
| AI3c(1) | Air Intelligence German Targets |
| AOC | Air Operating Company Wembley |
| | Air Officer Commanding |
| APIS | Army Photographic Interpretation Section |
| BEF | British Expeditionary Forces |
| BIGOT | Security classification for Operation Overlord |
| BODYLINE | V-weapons investigation |
| CIU | Central Interpretation Unit |
| COS | Chiefs-of-Staff |
| CROSSBOW | V-1 Flying bomb launching sites investigation |
| EOU | Enemy Objectives Unit |
| ETA | Estimated Time of Arrival |
| FW | Focke-Wulfe |
| GEE | Navigational Aid |
| GILO | Ground Intelligence Liaison Officer |
| GRAND SLAM | Barnes Wallis' 15 ton (long) penetrating Bomb |
| He | Heinkel |
| HE | High Explosive |
| IRLS | Infra-red line scan |
| IRFC | Infra-red false colour |
| JARIC | Joint Air Reconnaissance Intelligence Centre |
| JIC | Joint Intelligence Committee |
| JPRC | Joint Photographic Reconnaissance Committee |

| | |
|---|---|
| Ju | Junker |
| Me | Messerschmitt |
| MEW | Ministry of Economic Warfare |
| MI | Military Intelligence |
| MOS | Ministry of Supply |
| NID | Naval Intelligence Department |
| OBOE | Radar Aid to blind bombing |
| OVERLORD | The Allied Invasion of NW Europe |
| PADUOC | Anagram of PDU and AOC (qv) |
| PDU | Photographic Development Unit |
| PI | Photographic Intelligence (or Interpretation or Photographic Interpretation Officer) |
| PR | Photographic Reconnaissance |
| PRU | Photographic Reconnaissance Unit |
| RAE | Royal Air Force Establishment |
| RE | Royal Engineers |
| RE8 | Research and Experimental Department 8 Ministry of Home Security |
| RDF | Radio Direction Finder |
| RIC | Reconnaissance Intelligence Centre |
| RNVR | Royal Naval Volunteer Reserve |
| SASO | Senior Air Staff Officer |
| S/O | Set course |
| SIS | Special or Secret Intelligence Service |
| SLRR | Sideways-looking Reconnaissance Radar |
| SOE | Special Operations Executive |
| TAF | Tactical Air Force |
| TALLBOY | Barnes Wallis' 5 ton (long) heavy calibre bomb |
| TCO | Technical Control Officer |
| TI | Target Indicator |
| TORCH | Allied Invasion of French North Africa |
| Upkeep | Barnes Wallis' 4 ton (long) Bouncing Bomb |
| USAAF | United States Army Air Force |

# Index